I'm Somebody's Mama

by

Catherine Tyson

authorHOUSE®

AuthorHouse™
1663 Liberty Drive, Suite 200
Bloomington, IN 47403
www.authorhouse.com
Phone: 1-800-839-8640

First published by AuthorHouse   4/15/2009

ISBN: 978-1-4389-0658-4 (sc)

Printed in the United States of America
Bloomington, Indiana

This book is printed on acid-free paper.

Dedicated to Valree, Leroy, David whose absence in this world leaves an irreplaceable void. May the light continue to shine in the lives of those who were privileged to know you.

Foreword

Hi. My name is Catherine Tyson and I'm a single parent.

That's what it boils down to most of the time. The amazing thing now is that I feel good about that statement, because there was a time when I felt otherwise about it, sometimes apologetic, pitiful, or ashamed even, but now I feel like I'm on top of the world. I mean so far, I have had to go through most degrees of everything and have managed to come out of it smelling like a rose, well most of the time anyway. Not unscathed by any means, but definitely stronger, smarter, wiser, and much more appreciative of every single day and detail in my life.

Do you remember the *Rugrats* movie, the Paris one, where the kids were at a baby shower that the adults were having for Tommy's little brother and Susie was downstairs singing that song about "a baby is a gift, a gift from above"? Well, if you do, you'll also recall that good old Angelica was upstairs doing something and heard the song and when she looked out of the window, she saw Susie singing this beautiful, melodious tune with all of the grownups just swooning at this angel of a child. Then, in true form, Angelica yells out, "Who does Susie Carmichael think she is?" and promptly ran downstairs to out-sing her. Of course that turned out to be disastrous, but achieved Angelica's goal of getting the grownup attention off Susie. You had to be there, but the point is, maybe someone is out there thinking that about me. I mean who does "Susie Carmichael" think she is anyway, to write this book about herself?

WHATEVER!

Exactly. I feel the same way but, you know, what I have come to realize is that Susie Carmichael thinks she is something special;

well, not Susie but me, Catherine. Yeah, that's right, I do think I am somebody special. Well, maybe not me exactly, but the fact that I am somebody's mama, that is very special and also quite an honor. I feel like the Blues Brothers when they were trying to put the band back together: "I'm on a mission from God", they would say. Let me tell you, this journey I'm on feels exactly like that, seriously, and I want to share with all of you out there who don't understand what this is all about and tell you that we single parents are A-Okay. Of course to those of you on the same journey, to keep your heads up and just keep moving, without fuss or commotion, you know, like "there's nothing to see here folks," or "get back to your lives, citizens." I mean, we're just living, aren't we?

Let me begin first by telling you that I know a lot about a lot of things. My friends call me a theorist and I think that is maybe the best word they can find to describe what I do. Come to think about it, I guess I should actually thank them for not saying what they probably really mean. Here I am a qualified social worker and trained counselor with a bona fide university degree. People say I am actually quite intellectual and can hold a decent conversation on just about any topic, then again, people tell you anything when you're letting them stay with you for free! Hhhmm, where was I again … oh, yeah … you see, when I began thinking about my life I kept coming up with these different emotions, it was literally like each day was a different emotion that to get it out of my system I began to just write stuff down. Eventually it sort of became my cathartic journal.

You see, when you're raising kids on your own, there isn't much time for anything other than focus: Where to work, what to buy, how to buy, stop to fix that thing, take this one here, take that one there, well, I guess you get the picture right. So when I did get the time for anything, I was usually so exhausted and miserable from having to grin and bear it all day, you know, with that front that we can put up and then trying to be the happy, "I got it together" parent that I need to be in order for my kids to grow up healthy and well-balanced amidst the turmoil. My exhaustion became frustration and the only outlet I found was to just write and write and write, and through the writing, I began to see the ugly layers peel away. It has taken years for some of them to disappear but thank God, they *are* gone and as long as I'm careful, they won't come back. I got to tell you too that I kept revisiting my journals from time to time, and you know what I found? Somehow, every time I sat down with them, I could always see the humor amidst the pain, so I guess getting it all down on paper helped me to gain a different perspective, and I can only tell you that this was a good thing.

"What's your field of expertise?" one may ask, and forgetting any accolades and achievements that I have gathered over the years—because they are just gravy anyway—here's my answer to that question: My field of expertise is parenting my children alone! Period! That's my answer and I am sticking to it! Fortunately, I have been blessed to be doing just that for over twelve years. I say "fortunately" to indicate that this state of affairs is in fact a blessing and one I feel privileged to have been charged with—in spite of the fact that society has statistically deemed this situation to be so dire. Now don't get me wrong, I'm not bragging or anything about being a single parent, well not in the bragging sense anyway, and in no way am I suggesting that one should embark on this path by choice. Neither am I claiming to promote single parenting as an ideal alternative to a healthy relationship where there are two able-bodied parents. Let's not get delirious here! But I am acknowledging and claiming what is actually my state of affairs, and no longer will I hold my head down when I say so.

So I invite you to step on this ride with me for a few moments because who Susie Carmichael thinks she is, right now, is Tyson, Catherine Tyson, single mother extraordinaire and more importantly, I'm Somebody's Mama, and don't you dare forget it!

Ground rules

Before we progress, I feel the need to set some ground rules for your optimum reading enjoyment.

1. Read with caution as contents may be wreaked with sarcasm; a coping mechanism perfected over the years.

2. Review your own sense of humor; if it is nonexistent we may have problems, so remember to laugh!

3. Be aware that it is not you off-track—it's my mind that tends to wander.

4. Finish reading and pass on to a friend who calls you for advice about her life—and hope she will get the "subtle" message.

5. BUY THE BOOK!

6. Buy one for your friend; books are great gifts.

7. ENJOY!

Contents

PART I

Living the Dream

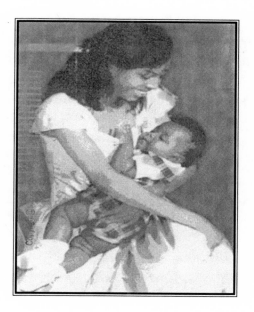

Dreams are images thought up in our head that appear to be the reality that we want to achieve.................reality is often just the opposite!

The dream of every young woman that I have ever known has been to be rescued by some dashing prince and live happily ever after. I mean, look at every storybook that we have ever bought or read for our little girls, from Cinderella to Snow White and even down to Shrek, for goodness sake! The stories talk about some great guy riding in to save a damsel in distress. There is always a damsel in distress and there is always some great guy to save her!

Well, my life was no different; I most definitely was a nineteen-year-old damsel in distress and my dashing prince came, one who would be my husband, no less, and save me he did. He saved me from all of the perils of the world, from the dangers that befell me, and, by George, he almost even saved me from evermore having to use my brain for anything again other than what he wanted me to do, say, or even believe! This "dream" I, of course, lived for many years to come. Thank goodness things changed over time and don't get me wrong, I was as much a willing party to this arrangement as he was and went along with it for quite some time before, lo and behold, a clue dropped out of the sky one day, saying, "Hey you, remember me?" As you can imagine, this was when all hell broke loose and then slowly but surely, so did I.

I think it came when I realized that I did not like someone telling me what I could and could not eat or actually forgetting that I had a "family of origin" before meeting him and now, all of a sudden, I needed permission to go visit them! I think the real clincher came when I realized that I had given birth to this big bouncing baby boy and was therefore deemed old enough to embark on this journey called motherhood; in fact I was even expected to be grownup on some occasions. I guess something got me thinking that maybe I should be grownup all the time if I had to be bothered with all that other grownup stuff like cooking and cleaning, keeping house, and making a husband happy which I'm sure he'd have lots of commentary on *that* one!

My dream of being "happily" married to my first love and having his babies could last as long as I went along with the program. Being the religious person that I was, I knew it was "for better or worse" and I therefore felt compelled to make it work. Yet little by little, I realized that it just couldn't and that eventually, this dream I was living was going to have to eventually come to an end. It was strange but somehow even then, I felt that one day, I would have to take care of those babies alone. First, there was only one and not long after, one became two. Where was I going, anyway? I was promptly reminded that no one would want me with "all of those kids anyway", and he did have a point only with a different spin. I do have to tell you that I left more than once and it was not an easy thing to do.

Imagine this: I had a husband; I was on the choir when I met him and all my Christian ethics dictated that I suffer silently. Plus, I was my family's shining star and how could I turn my children into statistics? There were already too many black men in this world that had not been raised by their fathers. I had to stick this out, grin and bear it, and appear to be living the dream. Leaving was not an option. I made my bed, now I had to lie on it.

I figured that what I would do was to start by educating myself so I could remain in my marriage, get a "good" job, and take care of myself and the children, since he was doing the basics. This was a good plan it seemed until I got to college and there were people there who actually thought I made good contributions, had great writing skills, and had something important to say, professors, I think they are called. I had entered an environment where people asked me for feedback and opinions. I mean, what was all that about? At home, I was a terrible cook and a mediocre mother who hated housework.

Somehow these two perspectives became confusing and incongruous to me. I had to figure out which was right and which was wrong. I think the negative one stuck longer because when you hear it enough it seems to fit so well, if you know what I mean. After all, I didn't like to clean the house, so I just did it to get it out of the way, and I got no thanks for cooking, so there was no love put into it. Plus, I had long been convinced that I wasn't smart or anything like that. Still, it perturbed me, until one day I got this mail that said I had made the dean's list and was to be honored with some others at a college function. As you can imagine, I was most definitely stumped. "Me?" was my first reaction. "There must be some mistake." Then, I found out it was bona fide and I was to attend the ceremony and receive my award. Needing feedback from my husband, I told him about it. I wanted to take him proud but the only response I got was, "I'm not going with you and I'm not watching the kids for you to go lolly-dollying in the street either."

Maybe I was on to something here. Needless to say, I went to the ceremony, took to the stage with one baby on my hip and the other screaming "Mommy!" in the stands, and got the first award that I can ever remember receiving in my life and one that would change my world as I knew it. I've since remembered others but it seems after having babies that close together, the brain just somehow becomes fried! I was now armored with the knowledge that I was, in fact, not so stupid after all, and I was at least good at something. I must also say that on that same night I found out that I would be receiving a scholarship for the duration of my studies—but only if I maintained a 3.5 GPA; sounded easy to me too at the time.

It didn't take me very long to figure out that this "dream" I was living was only a farce. I had a man—and I was lonely. Yes, I did have a man; I had a man who wanted to be away from me more than he wanted to be near me. I had a man who I had met in church but who now asked me to attend a different one from him so he would not be disturbed by our children's noise. I realized that I was a single mother even before I left my husband!

But as we all know, things have to get worse before they get better and sure enough, they did. However as I became a little more confident, I also became a little more defiant. I mean, I was an honor student and all; people thought I was smart, so at home I was not standing for all that negative kind of talk so much anymore. I started answering back and not "listening" anymore. I was driving a car once again, and visiting my mother, and eating curried chicken, and so on and so on ….

That was when the dream that I was living started finding me locked out of my own home when I got there too late (10:00 pm), locked out of the bedroom because the dishes had not been washed, and being told to get out on a regular basis. The dream I was living found me pregnant for the third time and on very shaky ground. The dream that I was living, in a word, "sucked" but there I was living in it—and growing more and more by the day.

Okay, so now I had 2.5 children, one year of college under my belt, and no job to be had in Dade, Broward, or Monroe County, and I was sinking deeper in the sea that I called my life. "Where was I going now and who would ever want me with three kids?" as my husband had aptly scoffed, I would often think. I therefore still decided that I would stay for the sake of my kids and I would stay for the sacred institution of marriage. The only problem was that by telling me to leave every day, my husband wasn't playing along. What was that about?

And on top of everything else, I observed my precious little boys beginning to speak to me like their father did and I had been thinking that I was staying for my children's sake! Now came another thought; maybe, just maybe, I should actually consider *leaving* for my children's sake. This dream I was living was going to have to change by default it seemed.

Making a long story short, six months after my daughter was born, my husband and I decided it was best for "me" to leave the marital home and rent an apartment. "We" also agreed on his monthly dollar contribution and shortly afterwards, with my baby daughter and four- and five-year-old sons in tow, I set off on faith, in search of a new dream. There wasn't time to look back or regret because I now had life by the reins. What I was going to do with those reins was not quite worked out yet, but I figured I would wing it, play it by ear until some epiphany occurred.

Little did I know the challenges that I would face on this journey....

1

Where it all started

On the quest to be great we must always look behind and beyond, all at the same time. A challenge you say, a must I say!

Growing Up

I came from a little wooden house on Walkers Road in Grand Cayman, with an outhouse for a toilet. Am I really that old? I never had my own room until I moved out of my marital home and even since then, I've been sharing with my daughter, now a habit for both of us, although no longer a necessity. I used to sleep under my grandmother's "sour arm," as my mom called it, and there was no place like that in the world. We had a dash window, which is a window that allows you to just pour the remaining water from the basin after washing dishes, a barrel in which to catch rainwater to drink, and pumped water from a well—and again I must ask, am I really that old?

The point is, I have not had much in my life from the very beginning, but one thing I always remember, is that not one day did I ever feel that I was poor. I used to feel sorry for other kids who didn't "have much" and my mother would always say to me, "Poor you, you don't even know how poor you are." I never understood that statement and since I never asked her to explain, I went right on feeling sorry for the "less fortunate ones," helping them in any way that I could.

I moved to Miami to live with my mother when I was nineteen, and five months later, I fell in love, at first sight, with a man who was the most incredible being I had ever met in my life. I married at twenty and gave it my best shot, but even though I was hoping for the best and trying hard to work out all of the kinks, those same kinks just seemed to have minds of their own. As the best was not materializing, I had to tap into that old feeling that I once had as a girl on Walkers Road. I had to revisit that child who saw the best in life, the girl who never knew poverty and felt lucky just to be alive. Finally, after my marriage crumbled, the one thing that I focused on was the need to succeed for my children. Defining what success was for me took a while, I admit, but afterwards, my plan was put into action.

I have always befriended the underdog and the point of this pondering is that from as far back as I can remember, I never wallowed in anything. I saw the goodness in my life and thank God, as an adult, that attitude has helped me tremendously. I did a workshop with a facilitator who used the term "attitude of gratitude" that she took from Oprah's O magazine. Honing in on that concept, I can honestly say that probably as a five-year-old child, I already had it and never knew what it was other than being my norm. Most importantly, as an adult, I still practice it daily. This makes me able to get up every day and be happy about my life and also to celebrate someone else's achievements and accomplishments because I realize it has nothing to do with me, it is all about them. An attitude of gratitude allows you to appreciate the situation that you are in and allows no time for envy, which will most definitely hold you back.

Another key factor in my life has been constant awareness: aware of where I am and how I am feeling about it. This allows me to consciously think about where I want to go and how I am going to get there. All I know is that when you start on that road, buying that new pair of shoes instead of paying the rent is no longer an issue because it is no longer an option. The point is being focused I was able to prioritize my life and then plan accordingly.

Yet looking back at my life and experiences I have to ask myself the question: "Am I special?" The answer to that is that I sure don't think so as I look at the road that I have been traveling. There are some basic things that worked for me that I can definitely see as being a catalyst for my results but other than that, I really think not.

The one thing that I know worked for me is that after I left my husband, I made going back to school my job. I had already started going to Miami Dade Community College and the academia bug had bitten me. Plus, I knew that an education could only help me on my journey. To that point I had three kids, no job, and one year of college under my belt, and let's just say the workforce was not out there searching the streets for people like me. So after assessing my situation, I came up with my plan. I made sure that the classes to complete my degree fit into my "mama schedule" and then any job I managed to get would have to fit in between those two. My kids were and always have been the first priority.

My plan meant my classes were usually held two or three days a week and work "happened" on the in-between days. Most importantly neither got off the ground before I got my children off to school nor picked up because they were, after all, my priority; what sense would it make to neglect them now, since "success" for me had everything to do with providing them with certain future opportunities in order for them to emerge as well balanced adults? In my mind, neglecting my children today didn't seem to add up to their success tomorrow.

I know this sounds a little oversimplified but believe me it wasn't. I had to make a lot of sacrifices and accommodations to make this a reality. I also had to change a lot of jobs to accommodate my plan but since school was the main concern after the kids were taken care of, school would be my ticket to success and well worth the sacrifice I thought, so on I would trudge.

Still, the road to success wasn't paved with smooth sand; instead, it was lots of gravel and rocks. I mean, from selling hot dogs on the roadside, and not in a bikini like they wanted, to waiting tables, and telemarketing in boiler rooms were all just a normal working day for me during those times. I even sold Avon products to welfare mothers who, I must say, were my best customers at the end of a month, thank you very much. You name it, and as long as it was honest work, I was willing to do it. I was not too good to work anywhere that I would not be ashamed to admit paid me. As far as salary went, I figured, "It's more than I make when I am not working, so why not?" What about public assistance you might wonder, well I was privileged to be on that for a minute until they found out I was in college and had a car and then was promptly interrogated and royally kicked swiftly in the butt to "go get a life". I am not kidding folks; that racket is a mess but thank God, I took my swift kick and on again I would trudge sorting myself out, armed with my blessed, never wavering child support that provided the security of keeping the roof over our heads and the utilities on.

All during that time I did, however, manage some so-called "good" jobs too (but these can be false security traps, I can tell you!). So although I worked at a bank as a teller and as a dental office receptionist and my salary at each wasn't too bad, they did offer the lure of putting off school. Then I would always think to myself, "Suppose this 'good' job does not work out? Then what?" So, again, on I would go with my original plan of completing my degree.

On a personal level, there were so many times when I had to explain to a man who was "around" at the time that added confusion was a luxury, that I simply could not afford luxuries; and that if he was not going to be part of the solution, then my problem plate was already filled! After all, my kids weren't an option, my education was my ticket out, and my job helped put food on the table so what other choices were there? Those really were the times when there was never a day without challenges, but as I look back, I realize that they made me what I am today. Now, I can seriously say that getting up every morning and being a mother to those three kids has become as natural as breathing. It is as normal as the sunshine. The challenges today are now manageable.

If you are a single parent reading this, then my words to you are don't ever wait for someone to help you figure it out; first figure out your goal, pray about it, then wait for clarity, which sometimes can take a minute or two, and then start moving towards it. However, always remember that you have more than you to think about so make sure you consider how that goal or decision will affect each one of you before making any sudden moves. In fact, even if you are *not* a single parent, these words could be for you too. They were foolproof for me.

Ah but does saying it make it real or is that often just the facade?

The Journey Begins

I know you must be wondering what happened when I got out there, kids in arms, dreams shattered, hope almost gone and needing to get it together fast.

Well "it was something else" is the only term that comes flowing to mind. Money was scarce, so we obviously weren't in the lap of luxury if that's what you're asking. Having said that, we did have an apartment in a good part of town, although the corners that I cut were in the luxury department, so we could look at the neighbors swimming in the pool at their nice complex, while my children and the others in the 8-plex were busy being hosed down while sliding on their lawn slide and having the time of their life. The other kids actually sometimes came over to our little festivities if you would believe that one. But inside the house was the worse for me because while looking around I had to accept that I had left a lot more than I now possessed, whether by choice or otherwise. I looked on the refrigerator one day and saw no "pecan sandies" and it brought tears to my eyes and a lump in my throat. These cookies that I did not eat and would never have an inkling to buy were, not only not there, but the reality that they would probably never be was quite daunting because they were the favorite staple of my husband's after dinner diet. The absence of those cookies represented my overall sadness as to my state of affairs. I think I walked around with that sadness for such a long time that it became normal to just be numb. The only thing that I ever felt good about was being a mother to my kids and the fact that I was intellectually capable of achieving academic success.

Men came and went, looking to make a difference, looking to score, looking to be friends, who knows the motives, but out of my mind's eye was always some suspicion as to what they would want with me with "all of these kids" anyway. I remember the man who hated my middle son and the one who hated my little daughter, little tyrant I think he called her, and the one who my little sister hated, wait that was all of them, anyway I also remembered the ones that hated me it seemed.

Jobs came and went; I quit some good ones, got fired from some, and went AWOL on the rest that I had no nerve to quit. I remember the days of little money and almost no daycare resources as a result, carrying all of the weight on my scrawny little shoulders and just simply being tired almost all of the time from having to do it all. The visits from my ex became less taxing and less scary because at first it seemed that he still "owned" me and would make all the decisions for my life the every other weekend that he showed up. Eventually, I became a little stronger each day, but not without its pains.

I was scared all of the time. Scared to leave the children for too long, scared to drive too far from home and at night, scared that someone would break in on us at night and I would not be able to protect us and neither would they and how that would affect them. I was even scared when people offered to help. You know I hardly remember ever leaving my children with anyone other than their daycare or babysitter; not even family members or friends were fit enough to watch my children for me. I sometimes think I studied Psychology and Social Work while at the University just to get a handle on my emotions. It seemed that getting a job after I graduated would just be a bonus! This fear kept me enveloped in a very safe place in my head where I could trust no one to not harm me and my children.

Most of the time, I walked to the bus with one eye over my shoulder, I drove my car just below the speed limit, and I made sure every thing was done by the book to ensure that nothing bad would befall us.

I looked around that little apartment and later the others as my safe haven; the place that I would use to form and protect these future citizens of tomorrow.

My story is not anymore profound than anyone else's but there are some twists and turns and some great moments of learning, growing and changing that occurred in my life that really made the difference. That fear I learned to overcome by prayer and belief that I was in control of nothing and no fear or hope could change that. I learned slowly that life is about good energy. I share some of these nutshell experiences with you in the upcoming pages so you can know that women are out here and proud of the valleys that we have had to cross to present the world with good people while becoming successful contenders in society.

I've said it once and I will say it again that being a single mother is an honor and if you have been honored to carry this torch, do so with pride because if you do it well, you are nothing short of a phenomenon and should be saluted.

But for choice:

Every day that I live and breathe as a single mother actually reinforces how not special I really am. I say this because as I work with others, I see that there are just a few things that separate me from them. It's not that I am any smarter, or have had better opportunities, or came from a family that helped me map out a future, in fact that may just be the contrary. It is simply that the choices I made were different, that's all. Maybe, I also managed to identify the opportunities as they came around and was constantly aware of red flags and gut feelings. In fact my gut refuses to leave me alone. It's always frantically waving and hollering for attention, a complete embarrassment really. I actually try not to go too far against it, if you know what I mean. So when my gut speaks, I listen!

I think it does simply boil down to choices because we all get opportunities, but what ultimately makes or breaks us is the choice that we make regarding them. To me, choice is the thing that comes with consequences and then elation or despair results from our ultimate choices. So I do believe that what separates me is choice. It mattered that instead of wallowing in the sea of despair that was my life, I was constantly trying to figure out how to beat the currents or ride the waves and get beyond that despair.

Don't get me wrong, I revisited that despair several times but I limited wallowing time and while I was down there in it, I always did, and still do, try to figure out how I got there, how to get out, and how to avoid returning. So, when I look at so many wonderful women, all filled with good character and lots of love for their children, I think, but for some choices, there too go I.

There goes me, with a man who is going nowhere and bringing her and her kids down with him, quicker than anyone can say, "He is a no good so and so."

There goes me, not knowing whether her children have eaten or bathed tonight because she is too busy trying to keep her head above water or seeking a man to help her survive.

There goes me, hoping against hope that it will all miraculously change when she least expects it.

There goes me, thinking that a fairy godmother and that ever-elusive wand will fix it all.

But instead and only due to the choices I made, here I go knowing that it's up to me to help create my own destiny with a solid plan, a realistic goal, a dose of tenacity, heaps of perseverance, lots and lots of patience, and a whole lot of prayer. And as luck would have it, neither of these benefits is exclusively mine; they are there for the taking.

Grandmothers—should we keep them? Is the verdict in?

Now hear this, there must have been a hundred times that this question has crossed my mind throughout this journey and I'm not referring to my own grandmother either. It's my children's maternal grandmother who is the "culprit" in question. Yes, you are correct in realizing that I am referring to my own mother, but don't get me wrong—if it weren't for the late pickups, the freak accidents, and the bad influence, she would be darn near perfect. In fact there was a time when I thought she actually was and that time, as I recall, was not that far away. My mom and I have gone through so much stuff over the years that I should find a term to best describe it. I haven't yet but whenever I do, I'll be sure to let you know.

I mean there was a time when she could do no wrong, but then again, there were times when she was never right. Plus, there were issues when it was always me in the wrong, not to mention the times when

I wanted to strangle her. I mean I would never tell her that because she would have floored me, of course!

But let me tell you, my mom was also a single parent of three for many years, and in fact, all the years I was growing up, I only remember her and my great-grandmother doing the job of raising us kids.

Mom worked like a bandit, cussed like a sailor, and defended us like a soldier. She could fight off any dragons, whether in the form of boys, men, teachers, or bad-talking family. She stood up for her kids on any front and always did her best by us.

My mother is so hilarious that my kids say things like, "Mommy, overtake that car like Grandma," or "Grandma would ball tires if she was driving." I even heard my daughter telling one of her friends while they were looking at our family album, "Oh, that's my grandma, the witch" referring to her Halloween costume of course. Then, whatever the occasion, she has some decoration to put in my house. This is the woman who lived for Halloween to take the kids out "trick-or-treating", rain or shine, and perfected her witch laugh to use as she accompanied them door-to-door. She had my friends laughing while I was growing up and now she has my kids and their friends in stitches with the same antics.

My mom gives me plants and cusses me out when they die, takes them back to her house to revive them, and then threatens me about watering them to keep them alive. Hey, I keep three kids alive, that has to count for something! Every pet that my house has ever had also originated at my mother's house because she insists that kids need pets to grow up with. Once I had thirteen cats at one time as a result, a long story and trust me, you don't want to get sucked into that one. She also drags second-hand furniture to my house and tells me that if I so choose, I don't have to sit or lay on anything, but her grandkids will not be on the floor because of my foolish pride. At those times, I don't think she ever noticed when her own refrigerator was empty since she was always so busy making sure mine wasn't.

But the rocky times were really rough and the day that I found out that she didn't have all the answers was really hard to get through. When you have to actually understand that your mother is human and makes mistakes is not an easy day.

But you want to know a secret? Most of this mothering stuff I learned from her. I mean, I also learned how not to do some things and how to get it right, but most importantly to always love my kids so much that they never forget where home is.

Yep, she taught me that and I am the better for it.

These days, my mom thinks I'm perfect and please don't tell her otherwise. These days are good. These days, I feel like that little girl who felt her mom's whole life revolved around her. That can't be all bad, right? So now, when she makes a little blunder, I see it as just that and move on quickly because, bad back and all, she is still willing to kick some serious butt for me. Now we just have to plan the getaway first because her feet aren't what they used to be, you know. She has always had my back and these days she reminds me that even though she thinks I'm perfect, we both should acknowledge that "I'm really not!"

Mom also tells anyone who will listen about these kids that I have, along with the other grandkids who are the best that ever set foot on this earth and she has supporting stories that she can share at will or on demand.

All in all, the one thing that I have finally realized is that my mom is my girl and no one, anywhere, will ever love me like she does. So I think I will have to say as the foreman of the jury that has been deliberating this case for a few years, that yes, your honor, the verdict is in. I'll keep her. I just keep lots of Crazy Glue in stock and close at hand so that whenever she does fall apart, like we all do sometimes, I can just put her back together again. Hopefully you are as lucky as I am to have someone like her in your corner.

2

"Bad" kids and all

Daily struggles involving precious treasures become bearable by a simple smile!

Just like Breathing

I know I said that getting up and raising kids comes in like breathing now, as normal as the sun coming up. Wow, ain't that something, just to be able to say that? I guess I must have forgotten those days of utter and complete tyranny, because I just watched a video from a few years ago and kept thinking, "Who are those people?" And I especially meant that sad, mean lady who looked no older than twenty-six but yet acted like seventy-six.

She kept saying stuff like "Put that down" and "Would you just listen?" or "You're going to break that, calm down now!" Those kids were running, jumping, dancing, fighting, and there was lots of screaming, from the adult that is, and I thought, "So they weren't the angels that I now think of them as being." Life is funny and the brain sure does forget a lot. I guess if you can go through twelve hours of labor and forget about that as soon as you have that bundle of joy in your arms, then anything is possible!

My daughter and I were watching the video because my sons are at that "cool" age and just can't bear to see themselves as whiny, corny little kids; well not all the time, anyway. But my daughter just loves to sit with me and watch the "little girl" that she feels so sorry for through the whole ordeal. "Poor thing," she says, "she's getting on everyone's nerves and no one likes her. Why are you yelling at her again?" In the meantime I am feeling so sorry for that other little girl that's trying to be so grownup and calling herself the mom with no sign of help in sight. I saw Christmases, birthday parties, swimming classes, recitals, graduations, baseball games, you name it, with three little kids, plus other people's, cause my kids don't seem to think three is enough for me!; one little mama and a whole lot of confusion with that one little mama trying to hold it all together.

Do you know what else I saw along with all of that though? I saw lots of smiling and laughing from those little kids as if they had everything in the world even though we were living in Dan Shaw's apartment in Miami or Ms. Linda and Mr. Tommy's house in Cayman. I saw those bad little kids being guided and corrected to do the right thing and even though I feel sorry for that young mama, I also can't help but feel proud of her. I feel proud that even though most days must have been overwhelming, see, I do forget, she never faltered. She never wavered, and you know what else? She was stronger for it.

Sometimes, I even feel sorry for the men that bit the dust during those times because now that I look back on those days, I can only imagine what they must have seen. I even remember some of them having the gumption to try to correct some of the "problem" things and I remember that li'l mama standing up tall and refusing to allow anyone else to chastise her kids. Now, I'm not saying that was right because as much as I would like to believe that all the men I met were awful, had ulterior motives, and ultimately did not want me with "all those kids," I have to admit now that maybe there were some good ones who might have wanted me anyway. I now realize that I was probably too busy doing it all or being too protective of my turf to even see their good intentions.

What I *am* saying, though, is that we as single mamas have to be careful not to allow men to chastise our kids when it's not out of love and be equally careful to allow men to correct them when it **is** motivated by love. That can get a little complicated, so I guess the only thing to do is listen to your heart and follow your gut. I know I let some good men go but I also know that I let some bad ones depart too, so maybe it all balanced out somehow, but I'm thinking it's always best to "err on the side of caution." Plus, my bad li'l kids needed me to get my focus straight far too much for me to be "lolly-dollying" in the street with some guy anyway!

3

Is there really a distinction?

Am I first a mother or first a woman, who defines it for me and however did we arrive at the decision.............

It's just not the same thing:

And here I thought being single and being a single parent to three kids was the same thing and wouldn't that have made things so much easier if that were true. I admit, it is mind-boggling at first but the fact that there is another word attached to the classification did kind of clue me in, just a bit. Yawning at the club at 10:00 pm when everyone else was getting down drinking and partying was another little indicator.

Here are my definitions:

Mother: Means that my life is no longer my own and anything I do from the day that I brought forth children will affect them as well as me. These facts govern my life.

Single: This blissful state means that someone is in total control of their own life, they make the rules, and they are their own boss. That fact governs their life. Observe the differences.

As a single mother I make no rules for my life outside of my children. Technically I am the adult but my life and schedule revolves around them from the time they marked their entrance into my world and from there on in. I hope I am not scaring anyone but if someone is a mother or father and have not realized this, I suggest they go back to the drawing board because something very important has been left behind.

Here is my gauge: If I find myself regularly at a party or a club with a halter top and batty rider shorts and can party all night, as opposed to yawning by ten o' clock in my Mickey Mouse pajamas because that is my normal routine, I need to check myself! So what that I still look good in a halter-top and batty rider shorts, I am somebody's mama! And dancing alongside some guy wearing the latest hip-hop fashion and hitting on young girls even though he is somebody's daddy! So I think we all need to just act like it. Yeah I did just say that; acting footloose and fancy free doesn't change the facts and not taking our responsibilities seriously is just not cool.

So in a simple answer to the question if whether there is a distinction then I think yes, most definitely and it doesn't mean that I am not entitled or allowed to live my life how I would like. It just should be with consideration for these lives that did not ask to be here and who I, like it or not, owe something to.

So before I look down the line of wanting my children to become successful adults I have to realistically and actively contribute to whatever it takes first. I mean it is all good to want my child to be a rocket scientist but first that same child needs to be up and ready to go to school every day on time and I don't know about anyone else but me and my young self feels like a crushed paper bag the next day after acting like I was supposed to be out partying with those other single folks. Plus I hear there is a law that back fat and cellulite need to be kept under wraps at all times or one could easily be thrown in the slammer.

Having said that ...

Even having just said that I think there is a distinction and the grave responsibility of being a parent requires certain things, there have been days when I woke up so tired that I wanted nothing more than to stay buried in bed. To curl up even tighter under the covers and tell the world to take care of everything that day seemed like a great plan. Those are the times when the kids refuse to wake up and get ready for school, the outfit I put on has a hole on the side, or my stockings have a run that I didn't see until after I got in the car. I forget my lunch on the counter and I am on this major budget where I can't afford to buy any—and all of this before 8:30 am. And on top of that, someone actually expects me to pleasantly "start" my working day on the dot.

I remember there was a commercial some years ago on television in which a woman was walking around in her living room picking up toys while asking herself, "Do I have to be a mom today?" Another commercial features a lady saying quite loudly, to no one in particular, "Calgon, take me away." How well I understood those women when I had days like that, one where I just opened my eyes and was immediately exhausted, even though I had just slept the whole night through.

Ever had a day like that?

But you know what the world expected me to do on days like that? Get on with things. Curling up in bed seemed so enticing but the only thing to keep in mind at such times was the fact that I couldn't even afford a breakdown, much less a break, so I had to just get up and keep moving.

Still, wouldn't it be nice if Calgon really could take me away, if only for just a moment? But come to think of it, Mr. Calgon doesn't even know the half of it! He would have his work cut out trying to drag me away from all the stuff that needed to get done; he'd be tugging for dear life!

So while I may often think longingly of that lady in the commercial, lounging in her bathtub, I also think, "Yeah, right!" It's okay to dream occasionally, but meanwhile, "I've got to be a mom today." And, on top of that, I also need to take time out to thank God for these days too because as I consider my kids I have to think; what other desirable alternative is there anyway?

What's another 1, 2 or even 10 when the house is already full anyway?

Yay! A vacation without kids:

Even though I accept my responsibilities with no objections, there still are times in my life when I just need to be Catherine, the woman, just that and nothing else! So when I turned thirty and earned my bachelor's degree, I felt I deserved to give myself the reward of a break ....

Memoir 1997, Carnival Cruise: There I was, all grown up and on my first vacation without the kids. Was I going to have a good time and let my hair down or what?

That, after all, was all I'd ever wanted. Just to get away and be a real person, a real adult with no yelling, screaming, or putting-on-guilt-trip-cajoling to get something. I mean, I was tired of doing that to the kids every day; I needed a break.

I was on top of the world. Two milestones to celebrate and I wanted to reward myself for my hard work. At that point, I had never left my children before and had only slept away from the boys when I went into the hospital to have my daughter. I had yet to sleep a night away from her.

Was I ever going to have a ball footloose and fancy free!

I had been planning my trip for months now and the time had finally come for me to go on my seven-day Caribbean cruise. Now, I realize that one week was a little bit ambitious, but at the time it just seemed right.

So, off I went on my singles share cruise. That simply meant that to defray costs, I would be sharing a cabin with another single person whom I had never met. I did tell you I deserved a vacation; I didn't say I had a lot of money or was "blinging" or anything. The sharing worked out fine because she was a day person and I was a night owl so we never got in each other's way.

They placed me at a table with seven other singles and there the fireworks would begin. I was the only person of color at the table, but that was not important, unless it explained why I was the BOMB! Just kidding of course and especially since there were three very beautiful Caucasian women also at that table. Let's just say we all were holding our ground, looking fine, and I added a little fire by cracking jokes and being sarcastic or maybe you had not noticed.

So there I was, sitting at that table, one of five roses with just three men. My roommate, being the early bird, ditched us after the first night, which narrowed the odds a bit more. I did not know then that cruise lines actually place you with like travelers. It was cool and since I was there to have fun and let my hair down, I can only tell you—the games surely began.

There was this one wisecracking guy, a New Yorker, no doubt, and he and I went at it. If he said, "Do," I said, "Don't" and on and on we went. He was following me around the ship like a lost puppy for the first few days until I almost got beaten up by one of the other females at the table, who apparently had taken a liking to him. We both were very afraid after that of even making jokes; I think she was a camp commandant or something! I, on the other hand, was simply being an incorrigible flirt and had happily been slamming the cabin door in his face each night, because even though I was there to have a good time, I was still somebody's mama and had to keep my wits about me.

Anyway, for the first three days, I sunbathed on the lido deck, even venturing out on the topless deck to be run away of sheer embarrassment at what I would be presenting compared to the younger, non mother like, silicone looking specimens, yep you are correct, I am hating big time! I basked in the attention of possible vacation suitors, danced at the disco, and dined on the delectable dishes aboard the ship. For those days, I had the disco DJ calling my name for requests the minute I walked in because, social worker that I was, I had already met half the crew and knew about all of their problems! And since I was so tired of being stigmatized as a single mother of three, while I might have mentioned that fact to one or two people, I had quickly moved on. I was just plain "me" on this trip and that was simply enough.

So, I lunched with the comedian, had breakfast with the band, went on the Mexican excursion with the Sous chef and maitre d,' and turned into a pumpkin each night when I fell into an exhausted heap in my cabin. I led the conga line, told men to go help their wives as they gallantly tried to keep me from drowning at Jamaica's Dunn's River Falls, and each day I thought, "This is the life." Of course, I phoned home each day that we went to shore and found the kids were all okay.

And then on day four, the strangest thing happened, I guess my breasts must have started to get engorged or something, I mean, she was only three years old, for goodness sakes, it hit me like a ton of bricks.

I had kids .....I mean, I ACTUALLY HAD KIDS, and I was away from them. I was not the footloose and fancy-free person without responsibilities at which I had been masquerading all that time, and my little people were elsewhere in the world, patiently awaiting my return.

Oh dear; there I was on a ship millions of miles from home, or so it seemed, and no way to get to the kids but wait for the next three days to drag by. The really bizarre thing was that for the rest of the time, I moped around that ship with this little picture clutched between my sweaty palms, to the point that strangers with whom I had partied earlier on became really concerned for me. "You have kids?" they would ask, amazed, and finally even the New York fast-talker managed to come to his senses and realized that the other woman at the table was actually looking for the same things as he, plus she ironically lived in the adjacent town to his, and he therefore quickly moved on. The other diners refused to stick around too, since I didn't drink, they said I made them feel like alcoholics, and now I was not even partying anymore. Needless to say I was alone ... alone ... alone, and all my good time friends had jumped ship; no pun intended!

I'm only kidding, of course, but seriously, the thing I had wanted most, to be a woman, simply a real live woman, had become old and by then, all I could think of was the comfort of being with my little brood. I finally realized that the thing from which I had so wanted a break was the thing that defined me for the rest of that trip. And what really felt good was just me knowing that I was not a member of the lonely hearts club because I had three little hearts that belonged to me, and that knowledge was worth more than silver or gold.

So, I hung up my disco shoes, dusted off my flats and walked the ship, impatiently waiting to hit shore and be back home where I belonged. Plus, I was so tired: I needed to rest my aching corns; my dogs were sure barking after all that partying! The main thing that I found out through that experience was that there could no longer be any such thing as me being "simply a woman." Once I had children, it seemed that I was "ruined" for all else but to hover over them, living and breathing for every little smile of approval that they gave. Catherine would have to find entertainment on her own time, not on DJ's, Richie's, and Caity's mama's time because she would be tied up … for, let's say, the rest of her life!

4

Making those ends meet

Counting those pennies and cutting those corners really does add up to the bottom line!

Repeat after me, "Thrift stores are your friends":

I'm not saying you have to like thrift stores and I am not even saying you have to shop in them.

All I am saying is that they are your friends.

I mean, when you can buy a Guess t-shirt and Oshkosh B'Gosh jeans for your young ones for a mere $7.00, these people have got to be your friends. … HELLO!

There was a time during my marriage when I was introduced to the *Red White and Blue* thrift store in Miami, by my Spanish professor, no less, and all I can tell you is that it was love at first sight. There were rows and rows of clothing from Guess and Oshkosh, to Ann Taylor and Liz Claiborne, all having been preciously and previously worn by some wonderful fairies who had decided that I could now have them for say, under $5.00 a piece. Now come on, who could resist such a phenomenon? All I can say is that store made my little ones and me the envy of the neighborhood while we were wearing the finest duds at the most affordable prices.

It even got to the point where I became a thrift store snob, looking down my nose at people who spent more than $5.00 on an item of clothing! I was showing off, eating at fancy restaurants, taking my kids on vacation, while my friends were busily shopping at the mall, buying the latest fashions with their scarce checks, just like mine,— and eating dinner at my house. Of course their children also ended up wearing my kids' clothing because the couple of outfits that $50 at the mall could buy were never enough. Oh, and the toys that we shared with all of their friends also came from the same source. I even picked up the hobby of buying cheap books from there so today I have a vast library consisting of books with minuscule prices stamped on them that I can't seem to get off no matter how hard I try.   These days I even try not to be too embarrassed about those tags, now that things are not so rough, if you know what I mean.

Do I still bargain shop you may ask? Absolutely! Did I eventually have the need and time for thrift stores as time progressed? Not so much because that is how life goes; we progress and are the better for it, but never do I fail to honor those days of sifting and "thrifting" through other people's discarded treasures.

There are some things in life that are designed to help us progress. I strongly believe that thrifty shopping is one of those things. So if you didn't know—now you do! And remember: If you are ever in a spot as I was, needing to make those dollars stretch … run like the wind to your nearest and dearest bargain center, garage sales count too, because someone is probably having a half-off sale even as you are reading this! Plus, think of it like this: You may even be embarrassed when you see that you have so much more money left in your pocket *after* purchasing your finds, than your friends who don't have the smarts to do likewise.

Am I too good to work there?

Generally we think that we are too good to work certain places, but I am here to say that if it means ah … let's say, eating, for instance, then maybe we should revisit our way of thinking.

Did I mention that I once sold hot dogs on the side of the road? Nothing is too "low" for me to make ends meet, granted it meets my criteria:

- I can hold my head up regarding the work I'm doing,
- The work is legal, and
- My responsibilities as a mother are not compromised!

Other than that, I don't see a problem!

Just recently to facilitate the purchase of my first home, I worked as a hostess for a restaurant. I had waitresses telling me how to fold napkins and how to set tables correctly, as well as telling me to stop eating the bread which was really, really good by the way. In order to take their instructions, I constantly had to remind myself not to mention my master's degree or the fact that I am a manager at my other job. Humble pie suddenly had to become my preferred dish.

Why that time around?

Because it was a means to the end!

During that time, I went home each night with enough gas money for the car, lunch money for the kids to take to school, and sometimes I was even able to buy a few groceries because grocery money was a bit skimpy those days and the extra money was helping to supplement a pretty basic budget.

Honestly though, if I choose to starve, get unnecessary public assistance, or let my kids suffer for pride's sake before I do an honest day's work, then what kind of statement would I be making about me and my priorities? Would I be "too good"? Or would I be running fast in the opposite direction? So don't be surprised if you see me in Foster's Food Fair or any grocery store in the world one day checking out your groceries; granted I will be a highly educated cashier but I'll be wearing a smile as big as the sun because *I do what I have to do to take care of my business.* When the choice is simple, the answer is even more simple … I am too good *not* to work there if need be!

So all you single mothers out there: If you are saying you can't find jobs and need public assistance, have you thought that maybe you might possibly be behaving "too good" to not work certain places? In other words, run, run, run; people are probably hiring at all kinds of establishments you've never even considered before. Remember that job could be just a part of your journey to greatness!

Prioritizing the bills this month:

A great question that often comes up in a single mother's life is how to avoid having essential services disconnected each month and the answer usually is just pay for them. And yes it is a final answer.

When it comes down to a new dress, a pair of shoes, or a trip to Disneyworld versus the children living in darkness or being without water for bathing, then the choice really is simple! Pay the bills. Always. It's never optional.

First of all, the roof over my head is essential. No questions asked. The how much, who's where's and all that other good stuff is merely just details that need to be ironed out. No one lives for free and if people think so then they are simply confused and I, for one, was always clear on that matter. Pay for the roof over my head because under the bridge, though alluring, exciting and filled with many thoughts of adventure might not have worked out for me and my little brood after all! And Mr. Electric Company is not a friend who is doing me some grand favor and Mr. Water company likewise. They are supplying my family with services because I have agreed to pay them for doing so.

Having said that, in my opinion and my home, cable TV is not a necessity and the telephone, especially a cell phone, is another commodity that we can certainly live without if unable to afford.

I also have some definite "should and should nots" when it comes to my children.

Should

My children should have lunch or lunch money every day; it's the rule that's why.

My children should not be regularly embarrassed by money matters because I should organize myself enough to ensure that they are not.

My children should feel comfortable bringing their friends home because if I want to know who their friends are, I must see them, noise, disturbance, empty fridge, and all.

My children should respect the fact that I "can't afford it this month!" I realized the significance of this the day when my five-year-old son held up a piece of candy in a grocery store and asked, "Mommy, can we afford this?"

Should not's

My children should never be allowed to have tantrums in stores because we can't afford something.

My children and I should not feel bad because I don't buy all of our clothes at the mall.

My children should not want stuff just because the neighbors have it and I should teach my children that by example.

My children and I should not go on vacation unless all bills are covered for at least the next two months.

The Tyson's are eating out tonight:

While I'm into prioritizing, I think it is also fitting to mention that any incidentals that were not a priority never took a backseat to regular family outings. My children are people too and they need to go into restaurants, sit down, and order like everyone else. I don't want to tell you how many young people I know who have not eaten at many other restaurants other than Burger King or the like. Hey, I get my share of burgers but fine dining it is not! The thing is, if my kids don't know how to read a menu and order from it or even which fork is for the salad then what world am I preparing them for where that stuff exists and I shudder to think what actually happens in that world.

I remember taking my kids to the Olive Garden or the Lobster Pot and saying before we entered, "Please act like this is not the first time you have ever been out in your lives." I would sit and let them all order and then get a salad for myself and eat what they had left over. Of course, when they were little, I'd even end up with extra to take home because as you know, small kids don't eat much. At that age they could order from the kiddies menu and so the total cost might have been a little over $35.00 even with drinks and tip. It might have been less depending on the restaurant and if it was in the United States; the land of the free and the brave or broke or whatever. Of course, I have since realized that this no longer works; my kids are almost adults now so these days I end up starving or having to eat cereal when I get home due to how much was left over for me to eat. But it got to the point eventually where I could actually swing ordering something for myself; imagine that.

I guess what I'm trying to say is that if I can skimp on the name-brand clothing and shoes and luxuries like cell phones for everyone and the latest video games, then I am able to help socialize my children to the worlds of dining and the arts, while at the same time spending quality time with them in other environments beside the house, where everyone is either tripping all over one another because of space issues or else tucked away in their own little corners.

I always try to remember that I don't just live to work, but I should also work to live. I take the kids on outings: Beaches and parks are free. We go for nature walks, visit museums and libraries, see art shows and plays. I look in the weekly entertainment column of the newspaper to see what is going on for free when finances are a challenge. I also believe in always including vacations in the budget and saving towards at least one each year. I shop around for what fits my budget and I just go for it.

What I've found out raising these three kids is that they are such amazing people and sometimes I miss that until I see them out in public, all dressed up like people where all the distractions of home and routine disappear. Sometimes I don't even recognize them all cleaned up!

How to make $25.00 feed you for a week:

There were times when I had to save every penny to achieve a goal but those were times when we still had to make ends meet. Back then I made a discovery: There is a conspiracy with the grocery stores. Has anyone heard? Seriously, those people expect you to leave every dime that you have in their stores. So the question is, do we really need all of the stuff that we insist on buying? I think not! I proved it by making $25.00 work for me each week.

For about five months, due to some financial adjustments I had to make, that's what I spent weekly, on food! You may not believe this but I literally fed my family on that amount. Oh, *and* I added the element of camouflage to it, too!

Imagine that!

Here's how I did it:

1. First off, I shopped by myself or with Merline since the kids and I just got sidetracked by snacks and ice cream when we went together.
2. I made a list and stuck by it.
3. I got the sales paper before shopping, to see what was on sale.
4. I did not buy junk food. Plus it's not good for anyone anyway so who needed it!
5. I didn't let anyone know what I was doing … I hailed everybody the usual way, smiling, honey … just smiling.

So what did I buy?

Rice	$2.39
Chicken	$3.30
Ground beef	$3.45
Frozen vegetables	$2.35
Juice	$3.95
Milk	$4.19
Fruit	$3.00
Water	$2.40

You are doubtless getting a little technical by observing that my list excluded cleaning supplies and toiletries, but remember, I said "feed" the family, so please remember to FOCUS and if all else fails, then improvise! Plus, I didn't say we were eating fancy stuff, but we were eating is what I am saying.

Plus, most important of all … I *prayed* …. He fed 5,000 with five loaves of bread and two fish, I was sure He would do as much for me!

Car woes:

Dear Santa: All I want for Christmas is a good, second hand, broken down car and one that is really affordable and will not leave me stranded again.

While pinching those pennies and watching that budget, one still needs to get around it would seem and transportation is a must when you live in cities like Miami or even the Cayman Islands. Whatever is one to do on a budget, well other than hire a rickshaw to be pushed by you and your little ones? Plus, they complained the whole way! Kids, I tell you! The alternative would be to get a car, but we all know how that can be. What looks good on a flyer or parked out front in someone's yard all cleaned up can suddenly look like its wicked stepsister when you become the lawful owner. Life is funny that way. Did you know that cars can have roaches? Stupid question, I guess, but at the time who knew? There I was, making my first real purchase; outside of the car I had at nineteen. Well my mom bought that one for me, so maybe it doesn't count.

Anyway, just so you know, I was coming from the days of driving my husband's old beat-up HBO van and lucky that he let me do so. Those were also the days when my first son, who was six months old at the time, would try to eat the pennies from the coin holder on the floor. I think he thought he was a bank, and yes he promptly spit them up as soon as he had his fill so we didn't have to cash him in, if that is what you were thinking.

I was also coming from an era **(1993)** when I had a **1977** Ford Granada that my mom had purchased from her employers for **$75.00**, yes; you read it right, seventy five dollars. And from which my older son almost fell out onto the street; he would have, too, were it not for his innocent foresight of hanging on to the door when it swung open while we were making a turn. Note: same kid, different mishap, but more on that on later.

Having come from those experiences and for sure, no one needs me to go back further, let me just say that me and cars just seem to have no luck, whether mine, mom's men's, or anyone else's.

Imagine my delight at having made this purchase of a 1987 Mazda in 1994. I mean it was practically "brand-new", so much so that I didn't even know how to act in that car! There I was, cruising along, feeling really good and proud, when out came some little friends from under the gas pedal. Go figure that one out!

That was just the first of many mishaps with that car. I probably shouldn't tell you about the time when the sunroof broke on the highway and right on schedule, it started sprinkling, a sprinkle that immediately turned into a downpour.

My little children, looking as terrified as any horror movie characters, were shrieking and diving into corners while I was valiantly trying to navigate that death trap that I called a car to safety. Wouldn't you know that the next exit was about ten minutes away and I had just picked up my nine-year-old sister from the airport, so I was coping with four, rather than three, screamers in the backseat! I did manage to find an umbrella to stick through the sunroof space though, which seemed like a good idea at the time, but did little other than to try and propel us into the sky---talk about making matters worse! I tell you ... Anyway, completely drenched and after much debate, we finally made a wise decision and abandoned ship, well, it felt wet enough to be one! We took a cab to safety instead of attempting any other stunts with the car.

Yet as I reflect, wouldn't you know, the one thing I remember the most about that day was how scared my children looked and how their eyes were focused on me, reinforcing the fact that they were all depending on me to make things right. It was—and still is—times like those that made me scared out of my wits at what I had been charged with, at what being a single mama really meant. But I digress simply for story writing purposes!

Remember the 1977 Ford Granada in 1993 that ejected my older son? You see the door was no longer able to lock; I mean it was an old car and had done its duty for society for goodness sakes. Luckily, being blessed with his mother's brains, he held on for dear life when the door swung over the street. He hung on so tight that we later found that the tips of his shoes were scraped almost right through. Meanwhile, my other son scrunched up really close to me while observing the whole ordeal—apparently he, too, had his mother's brain; what can I say. To me, all this was worth repeating because the moral that emerged from that particular ordeal is people; please believe what they say about car seats and seatbelts saving lives.

Time and progress wait for none so picture me driving in my nice minivan when out falls the window ... seriously. My "new" transport, about 5 years old, I mean practically NEW again, and something happened? Again? People undoubtedly wondered why I was driving around with a black garbage bag where the window should have been, but hello, remember the rain ordeal I told you about? I was shell-shocked, what can I say! What really fascinated me about this situation was the notion that my window could just get tired of hanging there and fall right out!

Then I buy my (fourth-hand) Geo Metro. My kids were mortified. How could I expect those boys, who were almost six feet tall by then, to fold themselves up and get in that? Of course *they* did not get the main part of my plan; after all, they were teens and totally into how things look to everyone.

I, on the other hand, had my focus on how the car would get us from point A to point B. My oldest son, who still usually doesn't say much, chimed right in true to form and corrected my statement: "Point A to point *scandalizing* B", he would say. Suffice it to say, we rode around for months, definitely squished, there was no way around that one. The kids would tell me to drop them off "down the road" from the function, or I would be looking like I was a crazy woman talking to myself because these kids were ducking down in the car!

So as you might imagine, I was constantly pressured to find alternate transportation, and it would have to be fast if I was to ever hold my head up in my house again. I saw my way clear and decided to ship a car from Miami (another ordeal). Just as the paper was dry on the transfer papers from selling my good old Geo, the other car, wouldn't you know it, naturally failed inspection and I was once again in a proper fix!

Having watched the Geo drive off without me, there I was, standing there "up a creek without a paddle," as they say. Thank goodness for a *Car City* loaner or who knows what would have become of me. So when you hear me say, "Geo Metro" days—you have no idea! Needless to say, my kids learned a good lesson too; they finally seemed to understand that looks aren't always everything. The lessons are always a bonus.

I really could go on with car stories but frankly while I don't know about you, I have definitely had enough!

5

All manners of Evil

*We love men, we hate men, but can we really do without them.......
and then what?*

Can you at least try?

Can some men maybe act like my kids are with me? It always amazed
me when I met a man who seemed to find it hard acknowledging that
I had some small very impressionable little people around me when he
was addressing me. And while my kids are older now, the amazement
still stands because it would seem that the antics just don't change. I
mean, I have to ask myself if men really do speak such crap in public

or whether I just carry a sign on my head that says "Game for crap" I seem to be such a magnet for men who'll say things like:

Me love you like cooked food—-Is this guy for real? I'm still trying to figure out how I'm supposed to respond to that one!

Are you as sweet as those grapes?—Does he not actually *see* my kids, or are they a figment of my imagination.

Whey me know you from?— Honey, wherever it is that I do know you from, I sure hope neither one of us remembers anytime soon.

All those yo crumb snatchers? — Yep, every last one of them.

True, it doesn't happen so often these days, I mean I am not as young as I used to be, or maybe it's that new sign on my forehead that says, "Don't even try it" Who knows, but I can tell you one thing—I'm sure not missing it.

So I would like to tell the guys that if you have taken a liking to Somebody's Mama, then my suggestion is to read up on something about women with kids and at the very least, stop talking to the lady's small boys about being "future heartbreakers" or "getting all the chicks at the party." For sure, don't go telling a mom that her little girl is "gonna be sexier than her when she grows up." Another thing, don't forget that if I don't want my kids listening to music with profanity, even if you don't understand why, then that means don't play it in their presence please. And for the love of goodness in this world, do *NOT* watch music videos that objectify women with somebody's preteen aged sons! It is just not an acceptable agenda item. Ok, so they might sneak around and do it, but just don't let it be with you!

You really do need to comprehend this point: Yes, a single mother might be sexy; Yes, she may "still" look young; But she really is first a mother to children and her grave responsibility revolves around shaping those lives and raising balanced contributing members of society. Respect her wishes is all I'm saying! And it doesn't after all matter if *she* takes it seriously or not; you have a duty to honor those kids for the love of humanity.

Plus that "macking" that you are doubtless doing is the same game you've used on other chicks and that is simply lame brother and if you hadn't heard, then go ask somebody please!

Married men:

However briefly, because we don't want to stay too long on this subject, let's consider the dreaded married man. All I have to say here is, "Kiss kiss, love you, but *I* can't go out every night—because *I* don't have a babysitter. *You* can't because *you* have a wife—and that really does not add up to one and the same thing! Now this piece is so simply written that I am truly amazed each time I reflect that it's actually just common knowledge and not some great mysterious revelation.

You cannot be eligible if you are married. There is no need for discussion on this subject.

Yet what is so interesting is that single mothers are such targets for married men; I have friends who are also single mothers and they all tell me the same story.

But listen, guys, this cannot work ... you are not a single mother's problem—and we are not your therapists. Plus "we is" people too and we want someone to come home to *us*. We also want someone to care that we lost a car in a natural disaster, let's say a "hurricane' for instance and to go out there and replace it for us! Now "I am not one to gossip, so of course you did not hear that from me!"

So if you have problems with your wife, go tell her about them, not me. I have my own share to worry about and you are of no help to me.

Find somewhere else to hang out, because I have enough drama in my life. Furthermore, you are not helping matters by having somebody's mama nervously looking over her shoulder to avoid being "clunked in the head" by an irate wife in the middle of town, while we are just trying to survive. HELLO!!

Oh and don't shoot the messenger because remember I'm not creating the news, I'm just reporting it!

Secret Acronyms (just between us girls)

YB....................Young Bucks (Simply irresistible)
BDP......Broke Down Playa (You know who you are)
OBDP.................Old Broke Down Playas (uh huh)
BPPS.......Broke Playa, Plain and Simple (Nuff said)
OTMM..........Old Tired Married Men (No comment)
YTMM..........Young Tired Married Men (Just pitiful)
OMM...............Old Mickey Moochers (Freeloaders)
WCST.....Working Class Snaggle Tooth (You heard)
BB...Billy Bob.......................... (WCST's cousin!)
STB....................Smooth-Talking Brother (Hhmm)
CP..........Commitment Phobic (Run, Forrest, RUN)
CTN.........Can't Take No (In other words … stalker)
AGNTS....Ain't Got Nothing to Say (Now you know!)
UBS.....Ugly But Sweet (Don't shoot the messenger)
NBF....................Nuthin' But a Friend (Poor thing)
TGTBT.................Too Good to be True (Believe it!)
TCFW...Too Cute for Words (I've got nothing to say)
TTA.........Too too Agreeable (In other words … liar)
JSTN...Just Simply Too Nice (don't smell quite right)
BJ.......Between Jobs (Why isn't he working again?)
SAM..................Still at Mom's (Nothing but trouble)
TTBS.......Trying to be Straight (Precious little heart)
TTFML.....Trying to Fix My Life (Who asked him to?)
TTFHL.....Trying to Fix His Life (Get it together then)

In other words, I have always had to keep all my senses clear when dealing with matters of the opposite sex—so I named them for quick reference when speaking with friends.

Lies and all that jazz:

Why do men insist on lying when we females can see the truth written all over their faces anyway? It is so crazy for guys to think otherwise because how we know they are married or already in a relationship has absolutely nothing to do with the imprint of the ring on their finger; it does have everything to do with shady behavior, though! Giving us cell phone numbers only, so we can "always reach them." I mean, who doesn't have a phone at home, anyway? That says a lot of things even if he is for real, one of which is that he is never where he lives, which we don't need anyway. And again, online daters, if he is already on the line every time we get on, well, who is he still looking for? It has to be more than me since he has found me already—but still doing the same things that he did when he was still looking.

Guys, we are not like Tom Cruise in *A Few Good Men*; we **CAN** handle the truth—and what's more, we recognize it!

Come on, all we have to do is pluck sense out of nonsense; if a guy has found his Guinevere, why does he have to look around the room and focus on someone other than you when he takes you out? I have such a problem with that. Why is he prowling on my time? I could have stayed home; *Law and Order* is on, you know! And guys, drown the lame excuses like, "Something was in my eye and I had to look away," or "I saw someone that I knew over there," or "The painting is so nice by the bar." It's all just lame. Have you forgotten that the last time we actually got you to an art show, you complained the whole doggone night, so what's up with that? And to top it all, enough is never enough: The waitress is always "so interesting," the checkout girl "seemed so familiar" the gas station attendant was "intriguing because of her accent." Plain old beautiful, exciting me is simply not enough on dates with these cats, but the part that hurts the most is that we don't do this to them and believe it, we have noticed, they don't have muscles like that bartender over there! Trust me you don't!

The last time I went out with one of those roaming-eye types who could barely keep his eyes on his dinner for "subliminally dining" with the blonde over on the other side of the room, I simply got up, walked to the back of the restaurant, and announced very loudly and excitedly, while pointing towards the window overlooking the water, that there were some over here, too, and he should come take a look!

Needless to say, he was mortified that I would do such a thing but no one was the wiser, which saved my face that time, and I had simply had enough. And granted, I never got another date with that guy again, but you just know how the bucket overflowed with the tears I cried for that great loss! And luckily, even when he put his foot in my back in front of my yard that night, I was still able to catch the end of *Law and Order* so the night was not a total bust!

If it wasn't for your children:

It should hardly come as any surprise when I tell you that men have presumptuously advised me that I might have had a chance with them were it "not for my kids." If I had a nickel for every time I heard that statement. Here I am, smart, witty, and funny as all get out; I'm nice, not so hard on the eyes, I have a job which is a plus these days, and—as long as a man thinks I am single, available, and childless—I am such a catch.

I attract all types, the good, the bad, and the indifferent, and in all age ranges. I mean, when I started college, I already had children and was fooling every young man for miles. Foolish me would get caught up in that whole mindset of age just being a number and if someone really loves you then kids will not matter. Eventually, though, I got told the old "if it wasn't for your children" thing enough times to just go militant whenever I met a man.

So picture this:

"Hi, what's your name?"

"Catherine, and uh, I got three kids, buddy, count em, one, two, three!"

"Okay, okay, I just wanted to tell you I have a UPS delivery for you, is all."

"Oh. Sorry!"

Then there was that one time when I got caught off-guard at a function when a gentleman came up to me and started talking. I immediately responded, "Look, don't waste your night on me. I got three kids and I am not going home with you tonight!" He looked at me like I was crazy but kept on talking just like he hadn't heard me. With that I simply took out my wallet to show him pictures 'cause you know a picture is more compelling than a thousand words, right! I lay them right out on the table so I can really get rid of him. Not missing one beat, he drags out his pictures of his five kids to show me! Needless to say we did have a great laugh about that and we went on to spend the rest of the evening discussing whose children were actually the worlds most brilliant.

My only problem was that he just wouldn't be convinced that mine in fact were!

Talk about assumptions, but at least that incident did make me aware that not everyone fits so snuggly in a stereotype, no matter how much we want to believe it. Of course, I also got to understand that there are some men who are just plain hardheaded, even when they're hearing the truth about the greatness of my children staring him in the face, it seems they are still not convinced!

PART II

The Dream Travels

They say that children are blessings and a gift from above; I guess those folks saying that weren't ever single and searching!

As I've contemplated this journey, I realized that even though the dynamics changed from day to day and place to place, it seems that all things still remain the same as the underlying issues still existed and often magnified or changed dimensions. What I did realize is that changes or not, I am a single mother, yesterday and today and although the young ones became not so young as before, the fact still remained.

I moved back to my home of the Cayman Islands a few years into the journey and, although some growth had occurred, I still had so much more to encounter. After moving to a small island, I found that the challenges were often unbearable. The lack of anonymity was one factor, the chauvinistic mentality was another, but please do not tell anyone I told you that ok. Let it be our little secret! I mean I already knew how much I would have to work to prove myself, but the challenges of being in a man's world, or needing to be old and gray to be taken seriously was a bit different after coming from a place where youth was envied and equal opportunity abounds. And I did say lack of anonymity was one factor; but did I mention the "who you know" aspect of getting things done?? Well you can only imagine if you have ever lived in a small town. The one thing it does though, is keeps you on your feet at all times!

I am that old:

Ask my kids, they'll tell you—they'll tell *anyone* even if they don't ask, but then I really do have to ponder the question too: I'm that old? REALLY?

"My mom is thirty-two years old and she works at Social Services," is what I caught my daughter telling some guy in the hardware store one day. I asked her later what he was asking her. She said he was telling her that she had on a pretty dress and she then started speaking to him about stuff!

Now how did my age and job get into that "stuff"?

That's what I'm talking about!

My kids have this bizarre way of telling all of my business in about five minutes or less, unsolicited! I usually catch it on the tail end and am sometimes embarrassed as to what information has been shared about me with an absolute stranger! And if I actually aged every time I hear that I am 32 years old, I'd probably be about 100 by now.

I've had to sit down with my children and say things like, "If someone doesn't ask then they might not want to know," or "Strangers are people that don't need to know any personal information about our family." They usually give the customary responses like, "But he was such a nice person," or just "WHY?" So I've since given up on the rational approach and have resorted to just screaming at the unfortunate stranger such things as, "It's none of your business" or "Leave my kid alone!" when I catch them doing the information supply routine. Oh and how was I supposed to know that the man at the hardware store that I yelled at was the pastor of my coworker's church?

A loan for a mortgage:

I've thought long and hard about whether I should include this experience. I've awaken in a cold sweat after finally deciding that good or bad, consequences or not I will. I am doing so because I think this is one of the dreams that we have as single mothers and are often times either deterred or put off, blocked or stopped; you name it. This was a turning point in my life and to this day it continues to make me proud to say that, yes, a "financial institution" and I own a piece of something that no one can tell me how to behave in. I no longer have to yell at my kids to not write on walls or stop destroying people's stuff out of fear but now purely out of care for our belongings.

A very big difference I can tell you. And as long as I honor my end of the bargain, it will be all mine one day. What a feeling!

Although a daunting task that I abandoned for a few years, I came back in full force and after ten years as a "renting" single mother, I finally achieved the luxury of home ownership. Now, what I had long forgotten, seeing how long this task of writing a book has taken me, call it nerves, fear or my little sister whose name is procrastination, is that this was the first literary piece for the book that I had actually written. I now remember being so dejected from being tossed around so much during that time that this provided the fuel for my bout of inspiration. So, if even for sentimental purposes or creative freedom, this piece I say, must stay!

One thing for certain was the road leading up to owning my first home was far from easy.

Do you know what it feels like, applying to seven banks trying to secure a semblance of permanency for yourself and your children, only to be turned down … each and every time? I did say each and every time, right? And I did say 7 banks? Just checking!

Well, it kind of feels like when you are checking out a new guy and trusting him enough to tell him about yourself, your weaknesses, your dreams. And then you begin to believe in him, because he's still standing there that's why! You start believing in his ability to understand what is in your heart and what you're going through and you also begin to believe that finally you have found that ever-elusive prize that has been your quest for oh, much too long—hypothetically, let's just say nine or so years, just to keep things interesting.

After all, he has to be "the one." He cares for you and all that comes with you. Wow, what a find. Your prayers have finally been answered, you think, and just after you have gone to that level with him (you know, "that" level), he's gone, out the door, with no explanation other than maybe he doesn't like the new plant that you have in the living room. Everything else was okay for him, but that plant—he just could not live with it!

Or maybe you have decided to go as far as that other level and just as you have disrobed, after he has helped you oh so gently and with such love in his eyes, he starts looking at you with disgust before hurriedly making excuses and leaving. You are standing there with all of your dignity just out there and you can't even move. You know you should, your brain is telling you to, but your body is just not listening. You feel paralyzed.

I know it may seem as though I'm digressing or at least creating a really harsh parallel to the bank situation, but humor me for a moment.

For there I was, *seven* different times, courted by *nine* different people. I was being treated like a queen, wooed like no other time in my life. We laughed and joked, had coffee and tea. I confided in them my deepest, darkest desires of home ownership. I opened myself, offering a piece of my heart and *all* of my personal information time and time again, believing that they would be good to me. And after all of that, only to stand there, "disrobed in all of my splendor," hearing them just telling me, "No. We're not able to approve this." No other explanation most times … just an apology. Sort of like the "Sorry, I don't like the plant in the living room" thing from Mr. Right!

But now, instead of being disrobed in the privacy of a bedroom, here I am, feeling like I am standing in the middle of town by the clock, for the world to see my humiliation. After entrusting absolute strangers with my life's information, the only courtesy that I am offered *seven* times is, "No, we can't approve it." No other explanation.

I mean, I still look okay but do I need to be standing in the middle of town by the clock, *NAKED?* I mean, I do have three kids people!

So here I am, a professional with a college degree and a steady job and no longer selling hot dogs along the side of the road. I'm making well over $35,000 a year and I **STILL** can't get a loan for a mortgage! And please note, my rent for the last two-plus years is way more than my mortgage would be and my salary would have been directly deposited into the bank, so they would "get theirs" even before I "got mine" and yet I still can't qualify?

What's up with that?

Wait, I got it. Instead of you taking it from me if I miss some payments, I might just run off with it, right? I may just put it in my purse and leave town, with no one the wiser … yes, that's it. I mean, come on, women can hold a lot of things in their purses, but a house? Or maybe you think I will strap it to my back, like a papoose, since I have so many kids, and run away with it. Well, there it is … mystery solved. What do you know? And why, for some strange reason, do the words, "Sorry, I don't like the plant in the living room," just keep resonating in my ears?

So, sir, now that I have done all that you ask of me, and now that I am convinced that you and I are right for each other, why do you stand there pointing and looking at me in disgust in my natural state? And, Mr. Bank Manager, why, in some cases, have you purchased the very house that you didn't know was up for sale until my application actually crossed your desk for approval? And why are you now renting it out to about ten different people and didn't even need it for yourself? Strange, all these mysteries ….

Hopefully, I will find some "maniac" at some future time that will not deem me a risk because I am a professional securely employed with a great salary. The maniac won't care that I didn't grab the last man off the street earning $2.00 an hour, clean him up, and get him to marry me, in order to "have a husband and security."   , I can't wait.

Hopefully this "insane" person will actually grant me the opportunity to pay their bank half my salary and three times the worth of the house over the next fifteen or twenty-five years. If—when—that happens, I might invite all of you, who pointed at me and laughed your butts off at the idea of me securing the loan, over to MY HOUSE for tea and cake, just the way you all wooed and courted me. But only if I'm nice, that is; and then again, maybe not!

Reality and the Bursting Bubble:

I realized that there are some basic things that you have to stand up for in this world, especially when it comes to being a single mother. Don't get me wrong, sometimes I lose my mind for a second and have to mentally recharge and regroup. And with days like the one I'm thinking of, it is of the utmost importance that I do.

Ok so I admit, I was kind of used to drawing attention from all types and this particular day I pulled up to the grocery store and fixed myself up in the mirror 'cause I didn't know who might be inside and I needed to be cute. I was ready to descend on the store; I'd fixed the strap on my sandal, my hand was positioned just so, my purse was over my shoulder, and I was ready for the breeze from the store's opening door, you know what I'm talking about, the one made by gushing air conditioning? I was all set for it to lift me up and sweep me inside where I would need to sexily fix my hair again. All of that in my "I'm not so obvious that I care" mode, "It's just that I'm still so cute."

And there he was and he saw me, too. He was acting all nonchalant like he was picking out grapes or something, but I caught him looking at me from the side.

I well knew the image that I was presenting … windswept goddess invading his world, swept in by a cool breeze on a sultry summer's day. I was silhouetted by the sun behind me, making the most of my image of youthful shapeliness draped in form-fitting pants and cute little shirt. Man, I could just imagine that I was nothing less than a mirage of cool lemonade in a scorching desert on a hot day. In unbelievably slow motion, I glided over towards him, of course trying to act like I got more than a lousy $25.00 in my purse. Just for a moment, I lost myself in his image of me; I smiled coyly, a smile that said I saw him watching me.

And right then, just when I just knew he was getting ready to make his move and I was perfectly positioned next to the kiwi fruit, all of a sudden there's a commotion and the next thing I knew, two boys, both taller than I, ran up behind me, calling me "Mommy" or something like that. … I forget, the vision went quite blurry at that point, distorted by preadolescent crackling voices, half deep, half high-pitched, half man, half child, you get the picture?

There they were and passing themselves off as the babies to whom I had given birth to not more than thirteen years ago; who, incidentally, I had believed would be picked up from music lessons in another half-hour. So why were they going on about having got a ride and "seeing your car outside so we came inside to find you"? No sooner did I feel a twinge of disappointment than I saw Mr. Cutie Pie's face drop like he'd been hit by a truck. He looked at my boys in horror and, get this, glared at me with disgust, as if I had just broken out all over in hives, I mean, wasn't I the goddess of just about one second ago?

But just as I caught myself thinking how much my kids cramped my style, I realized like lightening, "Hey, they are my style!" and I knew that when he and his cute picking-out-grapes-self went out looking for someone younger and cuter than me my boys would still be loving me like crazy.

So he could go on with his tired self!

Who wanted him anyway?

In fact, I decided to spend some of that $25.00 on what the kids wanted that day! I didn't need a man that bad, because guess what, they were—and are—my men and if he didn't want them too, he couldn't have me!

6

Friends and foes

Friends are people who know just the amount of money you have in your pocket in order to ask for it, down to the dollar, on a day when you had it to spare!
Enemies would never know these things!

Shaw's Goddesses

My first apartment must have been a God send because I moved into a single mama haven it seemed. I had neighbors from all walks of life that were on this same journey. I can't for the life of me remember how or where I stumbled on this apartment but I did and when I think back cannot imagine how I would have survived without the help of all of these wonderful people. We shared our stories and struggles, gifts and talents and made one big happy community. The memories we made there as our children grew and we progressed are priceless. I remember the antics of the neighbors who didn't like us or our children and chuckle to myself that as my children got older I actually felt the same way about other little kids but of course at the time was unable to see their reality. I had four wonderful ladies living there that helped me with my kids and provided such support that one day I promise myself that I will write a book about it.

You see we lived in Mr. Dan Shaw's apartment, what I call an 8-plex, four apartments on one side, and four on the other. Liked it or not, we faced each other daily. There was Maria from Cuba who, although could speak no English, baby sat for everyone. My daughter took her first steps in Maria's apartment and what I got when I came home that evening was something like "shoo dawdie walkie naw!" only for it to be translated by another neighbor, also Spanish who then told me "sho liddy gyir walk thoday" and that my friend was how I knew that my child had taken her first steps. Of course I cried myself to sleep that night since, not only had I missed her walking, but I still couldn't fully understand what anyone had said. Then there was Lilly from Chili who although was the hot mama of the yard, had three children, a heart of gold and man problems since he was always in and out of the big house and her parents, rich I was told, was calling daily trying to get her back in her country where she had left only to come to America to go to school and ended up falling in love with one of the USA's finest. There was Edith from Haiti, who had a husband that wanted to father all of our kids with the strap and was avoided except for holidays when he was jolly and nice, but since he worked so much she was almost always on her own and therefore in my apartment where her children wanted to eat because they "did not like Haitian food anymore since I moved in". And since our children were about the same age it just worked.

And not to forget, Xiomara from Dominican Republic, who was a Pediatrician in her country and because she could speak barely any

English was unable to pass the test to practice in America. She was the neighborhood's doctor and helped us through many a night of teething and ailments. Because my door practically opened into her living room she was my closest friend and partner in crime. We actually became undercover sleuths for all of the women in the neighborhood for a small fee; mainly chores or a particular dish cooked. We could find any wayward or lying man for miles, I mean different states even. I think they call that entrepreneurship these days. She had three teenagers who antagonized my little children daily and traded off with me to watch her teens as they helped with mine when she was working.

The old adage of a village raising a child was alive at the doorsteps of Shaw's Apartment. There were four other families who provided entertainment with their antics but until the book comes out, my lips are sealed as to the happenings from them but I can say fireworks don't only happen on New Year's Eve! Catholic girls climbing out of windows and ending up pregnant with no one knowing how that happened except us who were up late at night talking on the stoop, Jehovah Witnesses hiding kid's toys in shrubs and pretending they didn't do it when we saw them. The mentally ill son of a tenant peeping into windows to see folks changing our clothes and then we getting chewed out for calling the cops. You know normal stuff like that! As a single parent on the journey it is the little things that count and although we did not live in the lap of luxury, we were rich with all that mattered. Life, health, values and lots and lots of laughter!

Of course we could never admit to Mr. Shaw that his apartment was not the lap of luxury so we paid our rent humbly each month and told him thanks for allowing us and all of our rug rats to reside their on luxury lane!

Just Because I have three kids:

Okay, so there are friends and then there are foes but what about the friends of whom we exclaim, "What would we do without them?"

I just love my one, or two-offspring's friends who habitually drop their one or two kids off at my house. I mean, what are they thinking? I guess they figure that since I have *three*, I'm not going to notice their angels clambering up and down banisters and doing all manner of wonderful "evil" that my own children wouldn't dare do.

You have to understand; some time ago I was at the computer and I "heard" this wonderful sound coming from my living room. It was the resonance of well-behaved children watching cartoons and quietly commenting about the program! I was almost in awe of my kids and virtually wallowed in a moment of absolute bliss, counting myself lucky for having birthed such wonderful spawn!

Then the phone rang!

Now who would be calling me on such a wonderful, peaceful weekend morning, at just about 7:30? Who else but my dearest friend, asking me to watch her three, not **two mind you,** but three children, since her six-year-old stepson was in town for summer vacation!

Get this—*I* was to be watching them so *she* could get her nails done!

Well, wasn't that nice, huh? I should watch her three rug rats so that she could be pampered for two or three hours! Me, with my ultra-demanding full-time job, not to even mention the three kids that I am raising alone, minus anyone to help out on weekends so she could get her nails done! What's a manicure anyway......I forgot.

Can you imagine? To make matters worse, in the background, I am hearing a ruckus so loud that I can only barely make out what she is saying, so loud is the crying, screaming, and fighting that her angels are carrying on with. She even asked me where my children were; because they were so quiet, she thought they were still sleeping. I didn't have the heart to tell her otherwise.

By now, I'm cursing myself silently for answering the phone at all but it somehow seems as if my mind and my mouth are not connected because I suddenly hear my crazy self say, "Sure."

Can you *really* imagine?

Well, I tried to retract but I'm talking to myself because my girl has already hung up the phone. I don't think I've experienced such swift action since, well, I can't remember since when.

I immediately realize my mistake and am in the midst of figuring out how I can get out of this one when my middle son comes up to me and asks who's coming over. When I relay the story, he in his ten-year-old innocence says, "Mommy, we gotta get out before they get here! They are *bad!*"

Have you ever, in the history of the world, known a time when a normal child didn't want other children around? So now you can understand exactly what I've let myself in for!

Twenty minutes later the brood arrived and after three grueling hours of noise, confusion, dragged-out, kicking and screaming combat, and an empty refrigerator, they leave. My friend was so rejuvenated that she was glowing. Her nails were beautiful and she had even managed to get a mini massage while she was at it. I, on the other hand, had aged ten or so years and was barely audible when I said good riddance, I mean goodbye, to her and her crowd.

I know you must be wondering if the favor was ever returned to me, right. Well, I hate to say it, but no! And did I hear anything resembling thanks you ask!

Listen, friends, I like your children and I like you but I have three and although it's hard to believe, I *do* notice when yours are around so could you hurry up and collect them in the time frame that you said you would and don't act like you forgot where they were.

Who says three equals one?

Try saying *three* kids—and meaning it, then we'll talk! See how that number fits on ya, how it just rolls off the tongue! See how "three" makes the summer sun oh so CRISPY!

My friends with their "one-child-selves" love to think that their reality is the same as for women with two or more kids. I know no one made me have them, but give me a break! I mean, when did you guys ever offer to take all two or three of your friend's kids for a night?

Another question: How many times have you left your singleton at their house for a sleepover? Exactly … so you do see my point then? Women, and men generally, have no problem with one quiet little angel of a child but as soon as you add quantity, you add noise and more expenditures and people who would've normally helped out, in a one-kid situation, are now running to the hills for cover at the mere idea. I guess I can't blame them really because now that my brood is getting older, I look at little kids as "terminating noise boxes." Maybe it is because I'm shell-shocked by all the years I spent with my own little ones, but I'm pretty much reduced to a distinctive rolling eye motion if any little person is within arm's length of me, and misbehaving.

So go ahead with your belief that having one is the same as having more, but when you tell your date how many and his face drops like a ton of bricks, don't say I didn't warn you. Oh, and when you are dropping your singletons off at my house later for babysitting, just be thankful you don't have to put your money where your mouth is because, these days, if you had two, well, I'm just saying, things might have worked out a little differently for you.

My Nearest and Dearest

It took me a minute to think of who this might be. I mean I have so many fabulous friends that have been there for me over the years; through thick and through thin. But then I thought who has been there the most?

And simple, just like that, it came to me, who else deserves the honor of being called my nearest and dearest?

Her name is none other that Miss GUILT!!! But maybe you've heard of her. And if you are a mother I am sure she is probably right there beside you as you read this. This girl deserves honorable mention because she really has been my steadfast and continues to be my mainstay friend. This phenomenon reminds me of the song by the Dixie Chicks called Heartache which goes like this:

"Hello Mr. Heartache, I've been expecting you. Come in and wear your welcome out the way you always do. You never say if you're here to stay or only passing through. So Hello Mr. Heartache, I've been expecting you."

Well if I just replace the words Mr. Heartache with the words Miss Guilt, right there I would have described this journey as a single mother. Every waking moment of my life I have thought of what more I could or should be doing for my children. When they were little it was more time, as they got older it was more stuff. All in all it is always **more**; what **more** can I be doing for them and what less I could give up to make sure they have all that they need. So to my friend Miss Guilt I say is that I am doing the best I can with what I have and learning each day how to do it better. Each morning I wake up and think that today is a new day and a new chance to do it better and that better does not necessarily have to mean more. And then I say to her to pull up a chair because I've been expecting you but I do have kids to tend to so I don't have much time to waste. So make your point and then get moving!

Roadies

I could not forget about this wonderful influence that has walked with me along the way because had I not had them, well, let's just say that phrases such as "going postal" or "road rage" might possibly have been coined after me. These influences were with me in my home, in my car, and at my job and almost everywhere you can think of; they soothed me, calmed me, riled me up, made me determined to survive among the rats, but most of all they were my constant friends who never turned their backs on me.

The girls I am talking about are those who offered me the solace of music. I'm talking about the Mariah's and the Jill's. The Cee Cee's and the Oleta's. The Anita's, Mary J's and the Erykah's and the list happily could go on for miles. However, my mom used to joke about Tracy Chapman living in my house. She would arrive to the smooth sounds of Tracy and Mom would say, "She's back." This sister friend was in my car on the way to school and every time she released an album it was as though she had done so just for me. Seriously, ask anyone who knows me and they'll know about Tracy Chapman. Generally, they run away after I start to give them the Tracy tour because if you come into my life and say that you like her but only know about "Give Me One Good Reason," well, you are either a fraud, or you've been in exile for the past twelve years because that would be the only excuse for not knowing anything else she's done and therefore proves you need a "sit down and listen up lesson."

I cannot name a favorite song or album because they are all the best, but if you would like, my friend and I will sit with you and patiently work along until you too become a follower. When you were privileged to hear a choir consisting of two tenors, one second soprano and one alto wearing pampers, then you know you had arrived. My children knew every word to every song and would sing along on queue. We were not sure about a lot of those things those days, but we were clear on all of Tracy's causes with no question. People would get into my car those days and look with all incredulity at the fact that my children knew all of the words to each song. All the while I'm thinking; Yeah, of course they know the words! Between Sesame Streets' "Put down the Duckie" to Freedom Now" for Nelson Mandela, I don't know what else there was anyway. When the choir in the back seat rang out the verse "ain't no man, no woman, no beast alive that can beat me, cause I was born to fight" with the beautiful building crescendo, well who, I simply ask you, could not have been inspired to survive?

7

Above and Beyond

Everyone lives their life by codes; it's the definition of those codes that becomes tricky!

Let's backtrack for clarity purposes, before returning home, I had completed an Associate and Bachelors degree amongst the chaos of America with three kids and many insurmountable hills to conquer. I returned home to more challenges while entering the working world, full force, with qualifications in hand. I experienced many things, not least of which the message that those qualifications would only take me so far and I might have to accept that other opportunities might only come my way "someday" and with a lot of luck. At the point of realizing that I had, in fact, hit the glass ceiling professionally, I made a grand decision to get the heck out of dodge, and go get something more under my belt from, my dear and trusted friend, the world of academia.

The quest to return to America after a few years to take on a Master's degree was nothing short of insanity. The land of the free and the brave was still free, but brave I wasn't, and it was ready and waiting to give me the ride of my life, fear in hand and reservations flying out of the window. Only thank God this time it was not a 1977 Dodge Granada.

A graduate degree:

First off, I must say that I initially felt that a graduate degree is like the song "WAR": "What is it good for? Absolutely nuthin'!"

I also caution that if you happen to find yourself in my position, with no form of help in the distance and lacking any support system—that is, any with the ability to actually support your effort, as wonderful as stated intentions might be—then DON'T TRY IT! Now I'm not saying it's not worth it, but there I was, imagining the world would be my oyster and that the pearl that had eluded me for so long was just out there waiting and ready for the picking. But what one has to go through before "success" happens upon you is truly the trying part!

Okay, so picture this, three o'clock one morning, coming upon the nanny/domestic helper "escaping" through her bedroom window, after promising that she would be with you until the end and when caught she sheepishly tells you that she has to go care for her "young 'uns" in Jamaica. Yep, and you're standing there dumbfounded since this is the same lady who promised you that all would be well with said "young 'uns" while she traveled with you to undertake your grand degree task. So six months and one ten-year American visa later, it occurs to her that she has children. Go figure, the things one can forget!

Not to mention your very interested, exotic, and very foreign male friend who, while whispering sweet nothings in your ear, also appears to think that saying "keeds, keeds, keeds, all day long" is another term of endearment, together with other wonderful quotes such as, "Everysing is just purfek with us—and thsen thsey come 'home!" And all the while you're thinking, like, "YEAH buddy, that's about right: They live here!"

Well, of course, as you can imagine, these kinds of "happenings" mean that a lot of "housecleaning" has to be done. There's the nanny who cleans herself out and the exotic one who you are left to "clean out." And in such circumstances as you will also understand, there is little of that done in the house again, cleaning that is, if you get my drift.

But kids are so wonderful; they just go with the flow. I mean, you can bellow out stuff like, "Clear a path for me, I'm coming through" and they do! They don't complain when we're getting clothes from the "cleanest dirty pile" either. And when there is an unbearable stench, they help me locate the source. It is really quite supportive actually.

The only problem I can recall that we really encountered after the housecleaning effort was undertaken was that they would complain about food, I don't mean me not cooking, because they wouldn't dare do that, for they perfectly understood that that would not occur during that study year and that was that; I didn't have a lot of rules but that happened to be one of them and I take rules very seriously! Somebody's Mama would not be cooking! At least not this one anyway and then the neighbors didn't seem open to that proposal of cooking for me so on I would forge with buying take out...................

Okay, so we were clear on the cooking thing, but my oldest son developed a knack for saying things like, "Mommy, you have to get milk," or "You have to get peanut butter and apples." He had this really great way of telling me I "had" to get something, and all the while I'd be thinking to myself, "There are only two things that I have to do, buddy ...." And of course being the "good" mother that I was, I just ignored him and continued to shop when I had a moment or a good day, when the urge hit me, or when my stomach started feeding off itself—whichever came first.

And then my daughter, who at the ripe old age of seven could scramble an egg better than the next guy, would say stuff like, "There is nothing to eat, we have no food." And I'd reply that she was so scandalous and that there was plenty of food in the house." I mean there would be bread and ...pickle relish. I mean, what more did she want, anyway ... kids!"

Plus my middle son and I, who happened to have put on a couple of good pounds during this extended excursion into graduate school, were licking our chops at the very thought of a bread and pickle relish sandwich; hey, at least I had the support of one of them.

But all's well that ended well. I did get the degree after feeling like someone was strangling me for one year straight and I was ready to take on the world! Come to think of it now, I'm still not sure how ready the world was for me!

So J finally made it:

I got to spend one year studying, regrouping, rediscovering my children and their many talents, you know scrambling eggs at 7 years old and locating stenches, you know, the normal stuff. The place to be in is America, so progressive, so refreshing, so creative and accommodating to differences. I had the opportunity to be a part of a society that embraces change and innovativeness and then I returned home. Was I ever in for more fun this time around.

Here I was, all grown up with my Masters degree, just knowing that the world was my oyster, ready for the picking. Yep, I was grown up, at least it seemed that way. I mean the last birthday cake had a whole lot of candles on it, I mean there was barely any cake to eat and the blaze that the candles caused, well you get the drift, so I guess I was grown, is all I am saying. I also looked around and saw three children looking up at me, just knowing that I could handle anything thrown at me which for the most part I did. Of course, they were way more sure of that fact than I was but enough on that.

The real question here is why wasn't everyone excited about grown up me and my degree? Well, what I finally realized, years later after is that the work force is really not that excited about women, well, not as excited as they are about men, albeit they may be less educated, less sensible, less creative, you get my drift. Now I had heard the stories, yes, but I was quite crushed after getting that dose of reality. So I did find out that we have to work really hard to get taken seriously in a powder blue suit, but has anyone noticed how excited they are to see a woman wearing one! That double standard just seems so off!

Now, I am quite a serious woman at my profession and I don't play those little "I am so adorable" boardroom games, so I actually do get taken seriously for the most part. I'm sure that most men in the boardroom think I am a battle-ax, at least it seems that way since they ask me to smile more often where I just reinforce their view when I respond by asking them if someone told a joke that I missed or something. I mean, I work just as hard as some of them and harder than most, come on! Yeah, I also accept that had I played their little games, it may have been easier to survive, maybe for the moment, but would I have been able to face myself at night? I don't think so!

I know you women out there know what I am talking about. We all know of highly educated women being paid less than the men who are basically on the same level. Those women do most of the work, get the least recognition, are seldom taken seriously, and are being asked to "smile more often, while fetching coffee", yet they are also members of the board too! Well, I can see now what it all can boil down to once you have "finally made it." I mean, what was I thinking, anyway? But I have persevered against the odds that continue to tell us that we are lucky just being allowed to sit at the same table with all of the testosterone. At least they now allow perfume in the room and for that, I guess, we should be grateful. Meanwhile, I will continue to forge new roads to feminine success. ...in hope that one day it will somehow be even or at least close to it.

Baby Daddy Drama

Who dat is?

That's just my baby daddy!

Remember that guy who I talked about in the beginning; you know, the one I was married to and with whom I was unable to get it together for anything in the world? Well, over the years, we surely went through a whole lot of drama. Sometimes it was baby daddy drama, sometimes baby mama drama because, I may have been a "tad bit" not so innocent sometimes (note the halo tilting a bit for dramatic purposes). We fought tooth and nail about almost anything; out loud, in private, calmly discussing with fire in our eyes and playing the silent treatment game when all else failed.

The story should continue with numerous counts of casualties and much continued madness but, it would seem, that distance, years, mileage, and (I guess) life just have a way of sorting us all out because the story does not, in fact, end like that at all. Since leaving David and then Miami, for that matter, I was able to spread my wings and fly, able to be who I wanted to be and not feel any undue pressure from any force other than the one I placed on myself. By default, I guess, we had to trust one another to take care of these precious treasures while not in the same country and figure out how to do it effectively. I am sure we both have the scars to prove that we were at war, but as age comes upon us, scars should heal, and often, if we are fortunate that is, we mellow out and learn to just co-exist. David and I seemed to, in fact, be that fortunate; fortunate to have been able to separate the grownup stuff from the parenting stuff. From early on we accepted that we were not going to be together, come hell or high water, but we did have these children who we loved dearly and we just kept growing as a co-parenting unit. We also stayed family. We were connected by this incredible bond, and as bizarre as it was to understand why we couldn't be together, we seemed to understand the bond.

While I was in Miami studying, I found that I had someone in my life that was very supportive, both financially and emotionally. Over the years, I did most of the hands-on stuff, because that was how things panned out, but were it not for him, it all might have gone a lot differently for me and the kids. Now, don't get me wrong, he was a royal pain in my foot many a day, even the good ones, demanding that "his children" be taken care of properly and without incident or major scarring, and yes, he was very unrealistic when it came to how to accomplish all of that, but we managed to come to terms in our understanding of what needed to be done.

David was also so intuitive that he felt it when something was wrong. Seriously, every time something serious happened with one of the kids, I could literally wait for the phone to ring and he would be on it, inquiring about the day and events and eventually finding out that something was awry. If one of them was stranded, he would miraculously show up. If another fell and needed to go to the hospital, somehow he would be in the area right as we were about to leave. Even after we had moved back "across the water," he would call on days of mishaps, chastising me, of course, for not ensuring that the children were kept out of harm's way.

We had some great growth moments like that one and I can tell you, without him being in my corner and rooting for me while we both pulled for our team, things would have been that much harder. I called on him for his advice and opinion before making any decisions concerning our children, and every picture that they took, I made sure he got one of them because since they were living with me, I knew he was missing some great things and I wanted to ensure that he was at least a part of everything.

One day, much to my surprise, he asked me why I never gave him any pictures of me along with the kids, and I explained I didn't want to make any woman uncomfortable by having to look at me in photos in his house. His reply, in his quiet, matter-of-fact way, was simple: "If they are in my life, they have to accept that you will always be a part of it too!" That really hit me, because for the first time, I realized that he felt the same way about me that I did about him. David was my parenting partner and became one of my best friends, and I can tell you, when you have a good relationship with your parenting partner, the normal day-to-day struggles are not so bad. I travel this journey daily as a single mother, but I had a great support system, and although I sometimes took it for granted that the money would be in the bank each month, or that he would always be there when needed, I now realize just how *present* he was in our lives.

We got on with the business of raising our children to be happy, healthy, well-adjusted individuals who could love *both* parents without guilt. I am so glad that we did that together because today I cherish every moment that we had together as captains of our team and only now realize what a friend I had in the form of my babies' daddy.

8

I'm not desperate—not today, anyway

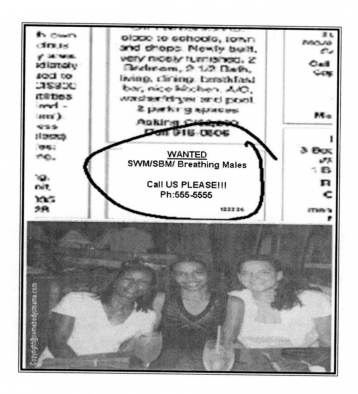

Desperation feeds a lot of things but the quenching of any of those things needs to be coming from the right place.

Social derelict need not apply:

This is a tough one and I'm not trying to hurt anyone's feelings, although I realize I will surely do that by default. So, please accept my apologies up front for doing so, but just work with me for a moment here.

Why is it that in spite of being reasonably intelligent and good looking, the only guys I seem to attract are those who look like characters no one else could want? Then after further research, why do I get proof that what started out as supposition is in fact SO?

Why does having three kids mean that I should be thankful that someone, anyone, even the dregs of society, has actually looked at me?

Have you seen me?

I look good! I know I do. As some people say," humble is so last year!"

So why does me having three kids turn me into this strange alien type creature who should just be grateful for any kind of scrapings?

I guess I do really carry a sign on my forehead that says "Loser Alert: or "Only social derelicts need apply"!

After all, in the normal dating world any woman who is good looking and is well-adjusted would never attract such deadbeat men, but once they know I have three kids it's like I am fair game. Sometimes I wish I'd just scare them off and they'd concentrate on avoiding me because when snaggle tooth approaches me I can only tell you that I am "very afraid"! Who then has the nerve to tell me that I am lucky he's even giving me the time of day!

If you think I'm joking, I can take you down to this place I used to get my car washed and show you a fine specimen, complete with gold teeth gleaming around the others that aren't even brushed! Then again, the huge guy from the local grocery store that my friend's boyfriend introduced me to one night at a party was a bit scary too.

I guess I'm supposed to appreciate the fact that they were willing to "work with me," having kids and all! Worse yet, I recall a 300-pound sweaty, greasy lawyer who I met at a party and had the nerve to snub me because he found out I had kids! Well, excuse me for living!

Don't get me wrong, if I meet a wonderful man who happens to not have all his hair, or is a little older than what I fancy to be the ideal age range for me, or who may be a bit on the robust side, then I will absolutely still be thanking God for sending him to me as well as the universe for lining up our stars.

You see, the issue is not the packaging that my blessing is in; it is more the presumption that once a woman has kids, she no longer has a right to even *dare* to expect anything better than flawed societal rejects. If anything, in my pre-kid days, I might have been better able to deal with "damaged" individuals; now, though, I have too much at stake—I have precious lives to mold and I cannot afford to take such risks. So if eating flies constitutes as one of your pastimes or you don't wash your hair very often, I'm sorry but this single mother of three is going to have to pass!

Lowering the bar on "low" maintenance:

You know what happens after you go through enough disappointment is that you tend to always be lowering the bar. One mistake that I found myself making as a single mother, ditto my friends who were/ are in the same wonderful boat, is that we all spend too much time seeing ourselves how we think the world perceives us. We should simply set standards for ourselves, live up to them, make no excuses, and just wait for the world to catch up, you know, a bit like affirmative action stuff.

But no, instead we waste a lot of energy believing that we're not entitled to demand to be treated like queens, which I consider to be fair since I know I am one!

We then find ourselves settling for all that is substandard and merely because we had the audacity, some of us, to have gotten married, had kids and failed relationships, or, in some cases, had the kids without a wedding and a meaningful relationship!

How dare we, huh?

And for those of us who made some bad choices but are coming up to the plate trying to get it right, well, the world is still intent on us wearing a "damaged goods" sash. Well, thanks, but no thanks! I made a new sash for myself that says, "Somebody's Mama" and it reminds me every day that the days of me "settling" might have, would have, or should have been long before I had responsibility for three precious lives, caring and nurturing, protecting, setting an example, and ensuring they are always treated with love and respect.

The day for me to settle is definitely not now when I am charged with such a responsibility.

Before that, I might have had time to work with someone and his issues, but that time sure isn't now because who is going to make sure that these kids become positive, contributing members of society, if I am busy working with a guy and his problems?

But before coming to grips with that concept, I too would sometimes be caught up with all-too-familiar "situations":

You have a job with the city—I hear they pay well.

You only have five missing teeth—that's not too bad.

You brush them four times weekly—I've seen worse.

You still live at home because you're trying to find yourself—you just need a good woman to help you with that.

You don't have car—of course you can borrow mine.

You don't want to go out to dinner because I cook better than any restaurant you know—Aww, what a *nice compliment!*

So when I came to my senses, I sure have ticked off a lot of men with my attitude of "Yes, I do have three kids—so what?" Why should I just be grateful that you will "take me with them"? Nobody's being given away, so where did you get that idea anyway? My mom was probably ironically the culprit. Being from the old school, she made the mistake of saying, "He'll take you with those three kids, so you need to stop being so picky." God bless her, she meant well. Luckily, I have brainwashed her into my way of thinking now. The story today is that I deserve the best even though I have a lot of nerve to expect it—so thanks, Ma, for the support!

Seriously though, one guy I know, who incidentally married a single mother, once told me in his great wisdom, "You got three kids, girl, a man don't even want to hear you talk. If he even looks at you you're lucky, and the only way to keep him standing there is for you to immediately get buck naked, rock his world, and then you just might have a chance." When I told him that was ridiculous, he laughed hysterically: "Well, you are going to be lonely for a long time!" He, I might add, was the proud possessor of ten good teeth; the others were either gone or rotten. Now why was he taken off the market, I ask you? What are the rest of us supposed to do now?

Watch out when the prince arrives:

There he was standing over by the bar, watching me like he had not had dinner and I was a steak. I admit I was flattered by the attention and even though my gut was telling me to just let this one go, I figured this time my gut would not win and I decided to "go for it." Now what I didn't know is that he had previously done a little research on me and already knew who I was. He knew I had a job and a car and, on top of that, probably even thought I had a place for him to lay his crazy lazy head.

But I have to hand it to him; he played it off really well. The charm was laid on thick and he looked pretty good in that red jacket that I later found out belonged to his friend. And the drinks that he bought me and my friends came from the dollars that mother or sister had loaned him to go out that night and keep him afloat till he got his last check from the gas station where he had just recently quit, of course! This too I found out later wouldn't you know!

You know how we women can get sometimes, instead of cutting through the crap quickly or playing that little violin that cares as soon as he opens his mouth, we become all googly-eyed and happy with that "Is this is it?" or "Is he the one, God?" feeling and knowing full well that Satan sends lots of stuff our way too. So it is quite sad after the roller coaster ride, to discover that he is but a fifteen-year-old boy trapped in a thirty-four-year-old man's body. I mean, I think that man is out there searching for his body, child, so you should give it back. Didn't your mother teach you to not steal?

My question is simply, *Why* does someone like this interfere with our otherwise together lives? Well, us single mamas, especially since we are just "a little bit tied up".

Is there something in his brain that says, "Now here is a woman who needs a mass of confusion in her life; this woman who has her act together just needs me to come in and help her realize what she is missing? She needs someone to eat her food instead of an offer to bring some over. One more mouth to feed shouldn't be a problem, even though I will actually eat two portions of what her children will.

"And she definitely needs me to visit her on her job during the day and talk; then I need to stalk her at lunchtime so I can ask who she was talking to at 12:18 this afternoon, in front of her office, seeing as I am between jobs and all. Oh, and let me not forget that she definitely needs someone to speak to her children in a sarcastic, childish, argumentative tone all the time, so that won't be able to figure out which is the eight-year-old, even though, technically, I look like the adult.

"And to top it off she most certainly needs me to rock her world at the end of every evening after having to endure all that other stuff during the day. 'Cause she is just waiting for that, ya know; to be held by an otherwise childish, nit-picking, jealous specimen of a man is just what the doctor ordered. But why she can't separate all that happens during the day and transition properly into the night is simply beyond me too."

But fellas, consider yourselves warned; the next time you see a woman like me, together and minding her own business that is, please stop and consider—and then start thinking that she may just be out of your league. Oh and try believing it and save you both the grief! She does not need *your* trifling addition to her life. Seriously!

And women, the next time you feel the three little words "this is it," and then you are just ready to say the other three little words, well here's three more little words for you: "Trust your gut!" and throw that fish back in the sea girl because the ocean sure must be missing him!

Red flags are just that.....

I actually don't need you to pay my bills—but I'm not paying yours, either! And does "Can I borrow $1,000 until tomorrow" have a familiar ring? And does tomorrow generally mean never to most men or is it just when one is speaking to me? I'm just checking!

I met this wonderful guy who treated me like a queen, I mean an absolute queen! He took me out to the finest restaurants and bought me the most expensive gifts at Christmas. I knew he was working extra hard for the big pay-off so I enjoyed every minute of it because I had something to prove also …. After all I *was* a queen and *deserved* to be treated as such, you know what I mean?

Well, he worked tirelessly to please me. He brought me lunch to work. He even ran errands for me. Then suddenly, I noticed a little change, nothing drastic, just minor things like he sold his car without letting me know. We were just dating so he really did not need to tell me of course—but seeing that he had planned on using mine until he bought a new one, well, that's where it became a little tricky don't you think? I mean, since his future plans involved the regular usage of my transport, then yes, I think I needed to know! But somehow, we couldn't seem to see eye to eye on that one! That was the first problem, but in general, he continued to be as good to me as he had been before so I kind of let that slide.

But then…….Somebody went and got fired from his job; I heard something about "a setup" and that his attorney "was dealing with it and he would be vindicated." Although, I was already thinking that this was a tad bit odd! Then, he decided to move back home to his mother's house, yet the one he was living in he had claimed belonged to him. He said he "decided to rent it because the rental returns would be more than if he remained there." (uh huh) He would use the money as extra income to support his new family if things "went the way that he was planning." Yes, he actually said that; much to my surprise too!

Then, "Can I borrow $1,000 until tomorrow?" also became a problem, especially because good old me didn't have the heart to refuse this guy who had been so good to me for the past three months! Yes, I *did* get my money back in the form of a check, but not the next day, and wouldn't you know that check bounced so hard I thought he must have been a star basketball player. Of course, there was a "perfect" reason and I did finally get the money back.

But later, still he needed another $1,500, because his mother "needed something." I decided that this guy was way too needy himself and that I wouldn't be the one accommodating his problems. Of course, I had wanted someone to love and care for me and all, but making me go broke was just *not* a part of the plan. And since it was now obvious that he lacked that little thing called security, I just had to cut my losses ... plus, like I said, I was broke anyway and certainly didn't need any more help in that regard!

What was I thinking?

I made a new rule and it goes a little something like this: If my car is in better shape than yours is, maybe we should just take mine and avoid all the heroics.

However, before I made this rule, just like most other women, I would therefore forge ahead on faith that things would just get better as the evening progressed.

Let's just call him "Mr. Impala"

Once upon a time, in a far away land and a far away time I saw, and heard, this big maroon Chevy Impala coming down my street with music so loud coming from inside that I had to wonder if there was a new nightclub in the area. Much to my surprise—and embarrassment—that disco on wheels was coming to pick me up! Sure enough, my friend was behind the wheel, coming to collect me for a date.

I can only tell you that there were no seats in the back of the car, just humongous speakers and the pounding in my ears was so bad that I promptly acted like his mama and told him to turn that radio down or else; I lived in a respectable area and all my neighbors who saw me and my small brood coming and going knew and respected the fact that I was trying to further my education while raising my kids alone. I wasn't about to let him change their minds about me! I even had a flashback, right there and then, to a time when I was waiting for the school bus and sharing with a neighbor my disdain for the car deafening music syndrome so typical of "young" men.

So much for flashbacks—and so much for "young"; did I mention that my ear-shattering Impala date was in fact some years older than I was and at that time I was already twenty-eight? Have I also explained that he had two kids and that yes, while he had on this lovely jacket and pants when I met him at a very professional meet-and-greet, such was now not the case? Same guy, different day; he now had on a football jersey, baggy jeans, and a back-twisted sports hat, whereas I, the "grownup" one, wore a nice dress and strappy sandals, complete with matching purse. I guess he matched the car and the bass blast, but as for me, what a waste of a good outfit, justified only by the fact that those were the days when I was still young and hopeful I guess.

Anyway, we eventually set off on our date and he reveals that he only eats at *Pollo Tropical* because he "can see how they cook the chicken there and he is very fussy with food." Now don't get me wrong, I love *Pollo Tropical,* the chicken grilling on the grill right behind the cashier and in front of your eyes is all very interesting. Seeing your raw chicken cooked to perfection in an assembly line format as you wait is quite quaint but I have on a nice dress and strappy sandals with a matching purse and might have been a tad over dressed to say the least.

So anyway, you guessed it; we did in fact go to eat at *Pollo* where he proceeds to talk incessantly with his mouth full and his hat firmly on. Of course, meanwhile he keeps telling me how "foine" I am and that he "don't mind the kids cuz he got two, too." After dinner, we go to a movie and I pay my share because he "hadn't realized we were going to eat so much at *Pollo.*" Remember who was the one eating incessantly with a full mouth and hat still on?

Still, the movie was really okay and we did end up having a good time after all. And fortunately, we both realized that he wanted a classy girl—but "just a li'l less classy than I was." What can I say—he had such a way with words! So, we boomed on home after the flick because the radio was "playing my song" and parted ways; no good-night kiss; he was, after all, nice enough to understand.

Plus, we did remain friends and I must tell you that if I ever needed a guy in my corner, he was the one, booming Chevy Impala and all!

Mr. Truck: Once upon a time, on a beautiful Caribbean island, not so long ago, I went on a date with a guy in his work truck, well, more accurately, it was his personal truck that he worked out of. First off, I barely fit inside for all the stuff that was on the seat; however, he did manage to clear a space for me, for which I should probably just have been grateful. Then, I had to go on memory of the road, because the dash and windshield were filled with every work order and newspaper that he ever put his little hands on. So there I was once again, in a nice dress, bad idea because the truck was too high to step up. I did have on more sensible shoes that time, though, so I guess I was learning.

Plus at that point I was well over thirty and almost reaching the jaded point anyway.

Yep, there I was, couldn't see a thing squished up against the door, praying that the lock would hold over the bumps in the road and wishing the date was over already.

What had I been thinking, anyway??

We forged on and then I thought I heard the truck starting to make this little sound but luckily, it was my imagination and we did not, in fact, have to stop to get water for the thirsty radiator or anything like you might be imagining at this point. Well, amidst the whole ordeal and having gone a little further, he saw a friend that he knew and proceeded to stop on the side of the road to say hello. He parked the truck, and me, right in view of the oncoming traffic, for the entire world to see, well whatever they could see of the top of my head, that is! I never thought I would have said it, but I thanked God for the paper in the dashboard, in spite of the fact that the pedestrians peering in were enough to provide the full report the following morning, seeing that I do live on a small island and since I was one of the town's social workers. "Who didn't know who I was, didn't want to know!

So then I waited and waited and waited for his hello to come to an end. I do believe that man forgot me in his truck; I guess he just couldn't see me and you know what they say about "out of sight." As you can imagine, the A/C wasn't working, so it was also hot. Yep, my hair was jacked up too; in other words, "I had look a pretty." So there I was, seething mad and no longer at *him*. How I could have done that to myself, I wondered? What was I thinking while he was clearing the seat for me to get in—had I really thought things would get better as the evening progressed?

And it's not that I was being materialistic, which he accused me of, of course, but let me explain that his truck had little to do with why I was so mad. The main point was that he had inconsiderately left me there for over twenty minutes while he said "hello" to his friend! Of course, his argument was that I was too vain to be seen in his truck; come on now, I was out with him; oh, how people can twist things to suit themselves. When I pointed out that we would never be able to take my children out if that transport was all he had, he "eloquently" responded that my van was big enough, and what would be wrong with us taking that? Okay, so our messages were crossed because we still failed to see eye to eye about him leaving me sitting there for twenty minutes. All's well that ended well, though; I got a ride home with some speed finally and we even ended up staying friends after much debate. Great guy, by the way, but I just couldn't get past a few things, old beat-up trucks that are a complete mess inside being one of them, especially considering there wasn't even room for me inside!

Mr. Jeep: So there's a jeep right, with a sunroof and a night that looked nice enough to go without the roof on, and instead of putting it *inside* the jeep we leave it in my house to give more leg room for the backseat passengers. Well, here I am again and you guessed it, once upon a time, on a night in the tropics in a far away land and not so very long ago! And yes, I did smell rain but since I am not a Navaho Indian and also not from East End (where faraway land's Indians clearly hail from), I didn't really trust my senses, so off we went, straight into George Town to the beautiful Pirates Week festival. Just so you know, this is an annual week-long event in the Cayman Islands during the last week of October, which is actually rainy season, but like I said, I didn't trust my instincts. Plus, it was an old jeep and the window didn't go down, nor did the A/C work, so having the sunroof off was actually a real treat on a hot night in the tropics. And even though my hair was jacked up again, the festival's street dance was awaiting and boy I was hungry and couldn't wait to buy some nice jerk chicken and cassava cake from one of the vendors who was selling stuff in the middle of the closed-off street which was a big thing, I can tell you. We got there; we ate and walked around, and had lots and lots of great fun. Then it was time to leave and we were on our way when, wouldn't you know it, a drop of rain hit my nose.

Nah … that was just my imagination, of course.

But was it?

Lo and behold, two more drops of rain hit me and although I tried hard to ignore those two, there was no denying it when out of nowhere comes a downpour resembling nothing less than a tropical storm, and well, I am sure you can imagine the rest!

There I was, holding up the sun visor over my head, trying to shield us, and all I could hear from him was, "Oh my God, it's gone down my back, I'm soaked." He kept on exclaiming with such incredulity that it was all I could do not to cuss him out. I had to concentrate on breathing, counting, and continuing to hold up that visor to shield myself; meanwhile, the blood was draining into my armpits! Have you ever held your arms up above your head for over five minutes? Give it a try and then you'll understand what I was going through.

Wouldn't you know that the stars were so out of line that night that we were stuck in traffic behind every other car in town that was also trying to leave the function. At that point, he was just yelling and honking at the traffic to move along and I just wanted to shrink to a pea in order to get through the whole ordeal. Now I did tell you that I am from a small island, right, and could only imagine how many people saw me with that madman, making a spectacle of himself; meanwhile, he was getting angrier and angrier. Now seriously, who cares who saw me anyway, since my focus managed to stay on trying to keep dry in spite of sitting next to a hysterical male who, instead of being apologetic, merely added fuel to the fire. I even forgot about shrinking into a pea for the agony in my arms; I guess I was too busy thinking of how difficult life would be after the amputations.

Anyway, traffic finally started to move and I calmly asked him to try to get us home in one piece. It seems that I have this uncanny ability to smell crazy really quickly and to know when to proceed with caution. A gift, you say again. A must when dealing with crazy, I say. Plus anyway, drenched as I was, I just wanted to get home to my warm, dry house and away from competing for the biggest idiot prize of the night, not to mention getting away from that guy. However, listen to me, he of course, didn't. What was I thinking, giving directions, anyway? So we ended up under a car park where people were up to all manners of evil—dare I go into detail. How could I have forgotten to tell you that before leaving town, my teenaged son and his friend had seen us and hopped into the jeep amidst the downpour? So they too were witnessing this whole asinine situation. Needless to say, I put my foot down about getting us out of that car park and safely home or at least somewhere neutral. Yes, you guessed it, I was no longer as calm as I had been, plus now I had backup rolling their eyes in the backseat and at the very least we could certainly outrun him!

However the best is yet to come as they say. Safely back at home after some more trauma with weather and jeep, my date proceeded to ask if he could come back to visit after he went home and changed out of his wet clothes! He had somehow calmed down and all was well in his world again---he had simply chalked the blunder up to experience. As usual, and since I was always a sucker for a vsad story, he did come back to watch movies and eat pizza with us, but date city was over! We did remain friends. Nice guy but for someone else.

Plus, I felt too betrayed by the jeep anyway.

No A/C, window not working, sunroof having to be left behind, come on, that did nothing for my social life.

And it called itself a car!

You can take the wheel, but you better know how to drive:

Speaking of cars and driving, it seems that regularly I meet a guy who wants to drive the car called my life.

But there have been so many times that I have actually had to think to myself that if someone were to be driving my car only to start swerving all over the road and up on the sidewalk, I would actually have to say, "Stop the car"" and tell him to get from behind the driver's wheel. So why in the world would I allow a man to take the wheel of my life if he doesn't appear to know how to drive properly?

I mean, there are men out there who are probably more screwed up than patients in mental institutions; believe me, I've met some of them. There are over-thirty-something year old individuals whose lives are in complete shambles and chaos, to such an extent, that he doesn't know his head from his feet, but *he wants to take the wheel.* Thirty-something year old, and believe it or not, I have even met forty-something's who are in the same boat, nothing to show for their lives so far.

Nothing!

Well, maybe a couple of children that they don't, or should I say can't, take care of, but nothing else; poor soul.

They barely have jobs and complain about that daily. They borrow money from people, which they proceed to spend with reckless abandon, for of course they have the best clothes and jewelry—but nothing else to show for their time on this earth.

I truly hope I am not being snobbish here, that I-and-my-three-kids-self am not expecting too much again, but come on!

I know it's hard out there and I know that life can throw us curveballs that we don't see coming, but does that mean that I should allow guys like that to drive the car I call my life?

So you can take the wheel if you know how to drive, but if I see reckless, crazy maneuvering as you pilot yourself along, then don't expect to take over my steering wheel; you best sit back and watch! You continue driving yourself into ditches and alleys, but meanwhile, I've got kids to get safely to school, or haven't you noticed?

Not desperate—But still with the questions:

So I won't let you drive the car called my life if you cannot navigate your own, and I know we women aren't desperate, but I often still ponder the reasons why we sometimes act so. Now, if I had all the answers, I'd surely share them, but since I don't, I can only say that I take it day by day.

And today is a good day for me. I feel happy in my element, thankful for my blessings, and grateful for life itself. Furthermore, I'm not focusing on anything other than being the best person I can be in this world.

What I also know is that yesterday, I was a little down about not having someone in my life, and the day before that, I wasn't too sure what was up. Oh, and last week I was feeling pretty good about being single.

So what I'm also saying is that I will continue to take each day, one at a time. No major plans or laments about lacking or not finding *anything*, love included. I am just happy to be breathing and blessed with an overflow of great things in my life. In fact, if that is all I've got, then honey—I've got plenty! Now, if you think that telling you where I'm at today means I've reached the end of my saga, think again! I mean who knows what tomorrow will look like? I'm just keeping my fingers crossed while treading the waters of life, and today just simply feels good!

9

You mean it doesn't get easier...........

Snakes and snails and puppy dog tails; that's what little boys are made of; Oh and cologne that drowns all perfume out and hour long showers that make everyone wait in line and so on and so on.....

Kids sure do say crazy things:

My kids almost always forget that their mother used to be an officer in the Royal Cayman Islands Police Service, but I sure take that seriously. I run a tight ship and I expect everyone who is younger than me and who calls me Mommy to fall in line. I will take care of you, feed you, bathe you (well, not anymore), clothe you, and look out for all of your needs. I wear lots of hats taking care of you, but I only expect one thing out of you: Never forget who the mother is; never forget who is in charge. Never forget that "I am the chick that pays the bills". Your job is to never forget those minor details, so even though now you look almost as grownup as I do, your job still is to have respect for me.

Simple really!

I will listen to you because of course I am from the new psychology mindset that believes kids are people too, but mix that up with good old-school notions and I call that a great balance. Even still, I'm sure that you will appreciate that there are times where kids regress and longingly compare themselves to their friends like these moments for instance:

Kid's Question: Can I go to my friend's house after school?

My Response: Where's his mom?

Kid's Answer: She's at work.

My Response: UUUUhhhhm, NO!

Can someone please tell me why my child should be at your house when you are not there?

Kid's Question: Why does he get to stay up past ten o'clock every night?

My Response: He's not my child!

Children need sleep in order to function. I need them to sleep to preserve my sanity!

Kid's Statement: My friend's seventeen-year-old brother is going to drive us there.

My Response: I am thinking NO again!

You've heard about the statistics, right??

Kid's Statement: I think I am old enough to do that.

My Response: Then when you have your kids you can let them do it!

*Oh, but don't you let me catch you allowing **my grandkids to do that!***

Kid's Question: Why do I have to come home before it's dark on weekdays?

My Response: Because I said so! (tried-and-true old school)

Whatever is going on after dark, my teenager does not need to be involved in.

Kid's Question: How come I can have kids sleep over but you hardly let me go?

My Response: I am not going to be able to explain everything to you!

I realize that seems like a cop out ... but it's just like that sometimes.

Kid's Question: Mommy, you know you don't want me to grow up, right?

My Response: I know it seems like that and you might be right, but I need you to work with me while I make the adjustment.

And yes, I really did have this conversation with my fourteen-year-old son.

Kid's Statement: He gets to have pizza every night and hot pockets and all kinds of fun things.

My Response: Maybe they can afford all that stuff.

But then, not everything is regressive and they do say other things like:

Kid's Question: You know, my friend always has fun food to eat at their house.

My Response: Well, maybe they can afford those things ....

Kid's Statement: But their mom is never home, plus sometimes I would rather have something cooked.

And I thought he didn't notice.

Kid's Statement: She lives in Patrick's Island. (very upscale neighborhood)

My Response: Now, you know her house may be nicer than yours, so ....

Kid Interrupts: Don't worry, Mommy, I like my life!

How dare I think she was so superficial?

House full of kids:

I don't know if my kids will remember, but for the past twelve years our house has been filled with other people's children. Our house is often a mess, the refrigerator stays empty, I can never get on the computer, my electric bill remains outrageous, and I seldom have one moment of peace.

One day, I thought I even saw strangers at my refrigerator, pouring juice. It must have seemed like an open house from the street and parched wanderers just came in and quenched their thirst. In true form, I simply reminded them that they should save their glasses for the rest of the day or put them in the sink if they were done. I do recall the older guy with the beard giving me a quizzical look, right before he shrugged his shoulders and drained the last of the carton of juice. Hhhhmmm!

You know what else, though? I wouldn't have it any other way. One thing for sure is that I always know where my kids are, or yours too, for that matter, if they are friends with my kids. As a parent, the challenges out there are so great and grave that you have to make sure that you know what they are doing, when, and with whom.

My kids get so embarrassed when I ask their friends who their parents are, where they are and what they do. Now that I am living on a small island again it is easy because I just have to ask now "who you fa anyway"?. But even when I was in a big city, I made it my business to know who my children's friends were and if I didn't approve, we talked about it. I think what has always helped is that we do have an open communication relationship in which we can really talk about things. Even though my kids don't always agree with me, if ever, they know that I have their backs. I am in their corner so they can trust my opinion; plus, like I've said, I am the chick who pays the bills, so I ultimately have the last word on the subject.

So, while my living room has never been my own because I allow every child within a mile's radius to come over and that means I have to give up some stuff such as privacy and a showroom house, it's well worth the price. And I *am* the boss, so to compensate; I have even broken the rule of no TVs in bedrooms, so I can have one in mine for my convenience.

So, if you happen to be looking for your children, chances are they are at my house eating cereal from humongous bowls filled to the brim with milk or drinking juice. Just call me; you'll see! Oh, and if the bearded guy belongs to you too, could you please come get him away from my fridge! I only buy enough for fifteen extra kids; so clearly, I have to draw the line somewhere! Plus, wanting to play video games all day at his age with teenagers just isn't even cute!

I am not your mother!

Speaking of the bearded guy in my refrigerator, I draw the line at being your mother; I already have two "men" that I am interested in raising, and it stops there!

I must tell you that my two boys really do have hearts of gold; they are so good to me and to their sister. Yeah, they can also be miserable, demanding, ungrateful and all that other stuff—after all, remember, they *are* human! But you can't find any better young men! My daughter even wants to know how come she can't meet boys like them at school, boys who are respectful of girls and are just plain nice people. There is no answer to that question, except to suggest that maybe they are out there and that when the time is right she will meet them. Hey, I can't traumatize her with the "real" truth just yet, right? She is still young and even I have to be optimistic! I said all of that to illustrate that the men I meet these days have qualities less desirable than those of my own sons and it's a bit sad that my youngsters are better men than a lot of adult males out there.

Even having said that, though, I am still not interested in raising any males besides my sons. So, if you are not finished "growing," you might want to go back home to your mom and have her finish the job because I personally have my hands full.

"Taxi":

This is who I call when a date isn't working out!

This is the word that I thought meant someone for hire!

"Taxi" is definitely *not* what I envisioned my middle name would be once my children became teenagers!

Did you know that ten kids can fit into an SUV? Now, I did not say *"legally* fit," so please focus! And if anyone has a problem with me having ten children in my SUV on a Saturday night, they do have a couple of alternatives. One is to let their teenager run around with other teens in a car; another is to go and pick your teens up from the movies like I do! Failing that, I will just expect a nice "Thank you for bringing my child home safely" from you.

Imagine me, fairly young, still technically able to "have a life," on taxi duty every weekend! It seems that my children think there is nothing wrong with me picking up their friends at 7:00 p.m. to drop them off at a function, only to return at 11:00 to retrieve them! Not to mention the fact that both my boys have different sets of friends to pick up and different functions to attend, yet it *still* seems normal to them! I would ask you what they think I do while I'm waiting to pick them up, but frankly, I don't think they care. In reality, I'm just trying to stay awake somewhere or possibly taking a catnap just to muster up enough energy to enable me to hit the road for them again.

Sometimes I wonder if they might be able to sleep on the sidewalk outside the function or if that would make me look like a bad parent.

By then I'm clearly more concerned at how bad I am going to look, rather than whether or not it would be reasonable for them to sleep on the street! Hey, their rationale has rubbed off on me, so what can I say?

So, I reluctantly schlep out to retrieve them and on the way home, everyone wants to stop at the local gas station to buy "must have" greasy chicken because they are famished! Mind you, it's midnight and no one is talking to me other than to make demands and ask for money. I am looking a wreck—although who's looking at me anyway—yet these kids think they're being reasonable while my idea that they should be made to sleep on the sidewalk seems wrong! You do the math! So there you have my typical weekend, all summed up.

Can you imagine what happens in my brain these days when I hear the word "taxi"?

Men: Why do we want one anyway?

You know what I regularly think about while watching those two boys grow up around me? Why do we ladies want one anyway, all grown up I mean? The scratching and burping, breaking wind, and spitting out of the car window, not to mention the bad breath; and that was all just this morning! I just know that grown men have perfected all of those little obscenities in life and get great joy and feeling of accomplishment when they do at least two of them very loudly and with special effects.

I have to wonder whenever I hear any of the twenty five teenaged girls who call my house on a minute-to-minute basis, if they are ever aware of what I am blessed with experiencing every day and if they were, would they still want these "hunks"? Well, of course they would, if only because they are the wonderful, smelly, loud little critters that we females apparently simply cannot do without.

And after all, they can be quite helpful when things need lifting and fixing, and they do take out garbage. Plus, most of the time they actually care about where I am more than my own daughter who, these days, is simply too preoccupied with the problem of me embarrassing her anyway. My boys are such treasures in my home and my life and having said that, I have only one wish and a last question on the subject: Why can't all men be as wonderful, loyal, helpful, and caring as them? Of course there is no question that I am, of course, a "bit" biased. But for the record, they are still loud and smelly; but oh, so adorable! And what would we women really do without them anyway??

Some things are not optional:

Let me see now .... Shirts, shoes, good manners, and school!

I am of the old-school belief system that there are certain things that are optional and there are those things that are simply not.

In my humble opinion, shirts, shoes, and school are some of the pesky things that are NOT. Little boys should not be running around without a shirt on a daily basis, and even though I am from a beautiful Caribbean island, they should also not be without shoes on their feet. I mean, I have seen the men who walk around shirtless and shoeless and "Frankly, Cinderella, it's not that attractive." I hadn't heard, but are ladies running after that sort of thing these days? I mean is it on the "to-do" list? Then, why in Heavens would I want my sons to emulate that sort of thing?

School, my friends, should not even be a question. If you are not near death's door, once again, humbly I say, you will go to school, just like I will go to work because I have my responsibility and you have yours!

10

Ponderings

Life gives some of us these little surprises, and if we are lucky and do right by them, they grow up to be big, wonderful packages, tied up nicely with a little bow, and God called them our children.

Things got easier after they got harder, and things became more manageable, after all of the chaos.

Pecan Sandies no longer make me sad. Can you imagine?

I am not so scared anymore, and bitterness, although it used to be a great friend of mine, I have driven off the ledge, but the work it took to get there was challenging.

I started out bright eyed and bushy tailed, hopeful and waiting to be filled with oodles of happiness that life had to offer, only to find that the happiness that I was waiting on was actually waiting on me to find it, and not the other way around.

Happiness, peace and contentment is deep in your soul, and when you find it, you can honestly say that the dream that you had all along may just need some amendments to come to fruition. But if it is yours, then it is possible.

My babies are no longer babies, and I often live in the past and marvel at how the time just flew by. But I am thankful of how things sorted themselves out, or to the little fairy that made it happen. All in all I've learned a lot along the way.

Note to self checklist:

I have made so many mistakes, too many to count, but as a result, there have been some things that I have learned that I call the do's and don'ts of my life. Almost like my "note to self" reminders that have worked for me.

My Do's

Do put my kids first.

Do prioritize my life.

Do live within my means.

Do be happy at other people's success.

Do set goals.

Do expect to be treated like a queen.

Do set boundaries for myself.

Do think about the consequences of my actions.

Do love my kids to pieces.

Do love my kids enough to discipline them.

Do pay my rent or mortgage on time.

My Don'ts

Don't allow my kids to talk back to me.

Don't laugh when they cuss.

Don't pierce my little son's ear.

Don't think beating my child is good discipline.

Don't let my kids call anyone else Daddy.

Don't cheat my children of having their biological father in their lives.

Don't introduce every new person that I date to my children.

Don't fall in love with a married man.

Don't think my heart always knows what my head is doing.

Don't buy my kids $100 sneakers.

Don't steal EVER.

Don't lie to my kids.

Don't settle for anything less than I deserve.

Don't buy a truckload of Christmas gifts if my rent or mortgage isn't paid.

Words to Live By:

As the years have passed, I've found that there are certain words and phrases that seem to recur in my vocabulary. I'm going to share some with you; for sure, they have helped me on my journey. I think of them as the words by which I live …

I might not be what you want, but I'm what you got: This is what I tell my kids when they start comparing me to other people's parents and the things that their friends are allowed to do. I explain that they might as well get used to it and work with me because I am sure working with them!

You may not have or like what you want, but you got what you got: This is my response to my daughter when she's constantly complaining about her long toes or the fact that she does not look exactly like me. And then I tell her—because it's true—"If we all could only have your problems," meanwhile rolling my eyes at her. What a gorgeous kid!

I limit my wallowing time: Self-explanatory? Wallowing is allowed, just make sure it is timed and limited!

Give me my minute: This can sometimes last for hours or days , and is actually quite hypothetical, but I need time, so let me have it in order to cope and deal with your issue.

I can always go back to my GEO Metro days: I truly believe that I should always be able to go back from whence I came, meaning to the days of being "poorer" than I am at any given time.

Don't shame your mama: I say this to my kids every time they go out anywhere. I try to explain that everything that they do represents our family, so they should try to ensure they are always contributing to our good name. If all else fails, I just simply say, "don't shame your mama, please!"

Of course, there was that one occasion when I had put on a skirt that seemed a little too short for me, but I kept peering in the mirror, trying to figure out whether or not I would wear it. My daughter, in her ten-year-old wisdom, scrutinized me and said, "Are you going to wear that?" I responded, "Maybe, I don't know. What do you think?" Looking at me very seriously, she simply replied, "I only got four words for you..... Don't shame your daughter!"

Keep your hands off of people's daughters: My boys say this in unison with me whenever I drop them off anywhere.

I am fighting the world for you kids and there can only be one winner: This is what I tell them when I have to put my foot down about certain differences or decisions I have to make regardless of who doesn't like it.

I can't raise a liar and a thief: It makes no sense for me to fight the world for my kids if I can't believe or trust them.

Those are the words I live by and I am sure if you ask my kids they would have a lot more commentary on them than I had.

Just listen to your gut:

Stop listening to your heart—it's such a pushover. JUST TRUST YOUR GUT; it's the only sane and sober thing in the whole operation.

I mean, have you heard the dialogue between these entities? The heart is going, "Oh, he seems so nice," while the body is oozing,

"Mmn, now *that* seems interesting," and the brain is half-heartedly cautioning, "Unh uhn, ya'll need to stop cuz that don't even make sense, it's not even foolproof." Meanwhile, the gut is saying in her still small voice, "Come on guys, we should be getting home, it's late." But who's listening? More often than not, the body is jumping excitedly, laughing, wanting to party and have fun, and the other entities are just so tired of fighting it that they just relax (other than the heart, which is feeling so sorry for whoever is perceived as the underdog that it can't emote straight anyway). Sometimes it seems like everything else falls asleep, leaving the body to its own devices, which is generally disastrous for all involved. Everything's left up the creek without a paddle afterwards. That's when you remember the dialogue that had preceded events, usually with regret, crying and cussing the fact that you should have had more sense and knowledge not to do certain things. So to be safe, in any instance that's applicable for you, follow the consensus: Just listen to your gut … it knows what it's talking about!

But still I ask, "Why can't I?"

Find a good man that is. I know that we as single women are sometimes so consumed with the desire to be in a relationship with the opposite sex just because of feelings of incompleteness that we can have. I mean, I suffer from the same syndrome and that just makes me wonder how much preoccupation our universe really needs. For instance, I imagine that at any given hour, thousands of single women are just sitting and wondering where to find Mr. Right and I bet that signals in the cosmos. Meanwhile, this can have his wires so crossed that he can't even focus on meeting us halfway! Think about it, a real case of "Malfunction Junction," signals going out and wires being crossed all over. How about we turn back to the old way of just waiting and when the time is right, letting it all just happen? Yeah, like we can think away our need for physical contact—sure, that will work!

But seriously, and on the other side of the coin, I have been thinking a lot lately. I've been thinking that all the time that we women, whether single or single mothers, you name it, spend lamenting on this great void in our lives, we are often missing the *boat* on some very important things that we do have. Here's what I mean.

Do you have a really great friend who you can call on at anytime and she will be there for you and happy that you called? What about one who is always upbeat and optimistic? What about the people that you are blessed to have in your life? I think about my friend who has known me since I was fourteen, and who today, could tell anyone many a secret that I may have long forgotten. She's my mainstay friend who loves me to no end and will knock you out if you dare say a bad word about me, well, she will knock people out for sport, actually, but I can tell you, she sure is my protector. She and I have laughed, cried, sang and danced the night away for no particular reason at all. Throughout my journey, she has been there; through the ups and the downs, the good and the bad.

Then, I think about my other friend that I have whom I met as an adult, and when I think of how sweet this lady is to me, I can't help but feel blessed. I have never heard her say a bad word about anyone, plus she laughs at all my jokes, so I have to keep her around.

There's my little sister, who is like a daughter to me; this kid is in my corner and let me tell you, she is such an informer that you can't tell her anything that does not get back to me. The love she has for me is contagious; she leaves me broke and with nothing to wear in my closet because if I have it, then that must mean it belongs to her. My brother "Neybo," who goes along with the program of the hour because he's letting me be the big boss, and one of my other brothers, who just thinks I am perfect. Of course, there's my mom, who is simply so everlastingly proud of me, and I have to tell you about my dear and utter confidante and friend who helps care for me and my children—not to mention my great friend who does security checks on all people coming near me in the form of a simple phone call and is so loyal every day that we breathe the air of this earth. And, I am happy to say, the list goes on of the wonderful people in my corner. Of course my precious and utterly wonderful children are a given in this whole equation! And dare I forget my wonderful South African sister!

These people make me feel good about being me, and if I spent more time thinking about the blessings of having them in my life, I'd surely spend less worrying about what I "need" to find. So lately, I have forgotten about Mr. Right and anyway, I know he's desperately trying to find me through all of those crossed signals and when we all ease up, he will come.

So please, for all of our sakes, get your focus off the messages sent through the universe. Do us all a favor and think about your support system and the people who love you and see how you fare off. I bet you'll find you are a lot better off than you even imagined.

Plus for the rest of the week at 8:00 p.m. SHARP, I will expect to get through, so ladies, please stop clogging up the system!

11

In the presence of Angels

The sweet smell of success comes in many different forms, some of which are right under our nose, where smell originates......go figure!

It's good when your children are wonderful:

Seriously, it does work out good when you have really wonderful kids. Mine are such troopers; they allowed me to drag them halfway around the world in search of my own dreams and they just trusted me. Yep, that's the only way to describe it.

They simply just trust me.

They trust that I know what I'm doing and they trust that I will always take care of them. They look me in the eye and just seem to know that everything will always be okay as long as I'm at the wheel. To honor that trust, I in turn have really tried not to fall apart too much while they're watching, to avoid freaking them out, you know or just enough just so they know that it is all right to fall apart every once in a while and "pick yourself up, dust yourself off, and start all over again."

Some of my special memories of each of my children are sweet and personal.

Little Man

I remember one day when my older son was about three years old and I was reversing the car in the yard. I had told him to wait while I parked the car on the side. He kept running after the car and I would have to stop reversing each time he got close. I finally stopped, looked him earnestly in the eyes, and said, "You have to trust me, I'm not going anywhere, I'm just putting the car over there, and I will come back. Trust me, okay?" When I put the car in reverse and started moving again, sure enough, there he was running after the car, but this time he was shouting, "I trust you, Mommy, I'm trusting you, okay?" Yet, he was still running after the car. That is so characteristic of him, "trusting" me but needing to have me in sight the whole time. I guess the "I'll trust her as far as I can see her" saying would apply even to me, except for the fortunate fact that he regards me as "Queen of the World," of course.

Another thing with him is that whenever we are watching TV or the whole family is together in one room, he never pushes his way in; instead he will lay down with his pillow, somewhere very close to where the action is. It's as though his safety lies in just being near and connected to a part of everything but not necessarily to be in the middle. He is the musical genius in the group and could play the piano by ear from the time he was about three years old. He sets his alarm and gets up every morning to take care of what needs to be done. He is the one who allows me to make his grownup choices because he just can't seem to be bothered with all that decision-making. Yet, he is also the one who knows exactly what is going on at all times, observing everything while saying few words. He is the most like me and the most like his father, all at the same time. Quiet but very intuitive. When he speaks, it is often times to voice the most profound of statements. All I can simply say is what a guy!

The Boss

I remember this time when we picked up a hitchhiker (in the Cayman Islands, of course). My two sons, who were three and four at the time, were sitting in front and so the hitcher got into the back. Well, my younger son immediately said, "Hi." and when the lady answered, she also expressed surprise because she hadn't realized that someone else was there. He proceeded to tell her, "Yes, it's me and my brother." She then asked if they were twins. "No," he said, "he's older than me, but everyone thinks we're twins." He went on to tell her his own name and his brother's name. At that point the lady asked him if the other one was unable to talk. In true form the younger one responded by answering, matter-of-factly, that his brother could talk. He then proceeded to call his brother's name a few times; the older one just slowly looked over and just kind of growled, "*What?*" Not missing a beat, the younger one said, "See he can talk, he just doesn't want to." That comment, in one simple sentence, described both children to a tee: One can talk, he just doesn't want to, while the other is the vocal representative for the duo. My little man, as ambassador for the Tyson family, came through once again with flying colors; the other one, who can talk, when he wants to, was quite happy to let him!

He never misses an opportunity to kiss me or hug me all through the day, but especially before he goes to sleep, he used to have this favorite saying when he was younger, "Don't forget to pray", one I could always look forward to hearing. He is the child who will always squeeze his way into the middle of wherever the action is. Not so much forcefully, but rather as a way of saying, "I belong here, right in the center of the action." Yet, he is also very protective of me and my space. He is the one who screens my calls, although my friends don't realize that that is what he is doing, and he is the one who checks to see what I'm wearing to go out, to approve or otherwise. After all, he's the man of the house he thinks! He keeps us on our toes with his wit and intellect, not to mention his noise. He is the most caring soul, the social worker I think, who always brings every stray home be it animal or human. A heart of gold, I call one the boss!

The Precious Angel

My daughter has always been Miss Organized. Since she was a little girl, she "knew how to cook": cans of spaghetti, heated and simmered at a low boil and prepared so delicately by the chef's hand for dinner, she even adds onions and green peppers to the dish now, or her special dessert made from cream cheese, bread, and cinnamon, which she saw on Nickelodeon or one of those channels. She makes sure that she brings her letters home from school on the same day and orders her books on time, driving me crazy with all of the details, of course, and she always does homework without me ever having to tell her.

This little lady has always had all the logic in the world; she's another one who is never anywhere but in the middle because, "hey, it's just my place and I know it!" I'm working on that attitude, but it is a little difficult not to indulge it since she *is,* after all, "third time lucky" since I did end up not getting another boy. ... Other phrases that were found in her six-year-old repertoire ranged from "This is not appropriate" to "I am not prepared for that." Oh and she *still* hates me to tell anyone "her business" so don't tell her I've told you any of this!

Anyway, years ago, one night when I asked her to hug me while we were drifting off to sleep, all just for her comfort, of course, she said, "Mommy, you know this is getting to be a regular thing, and it is not the easiest job in the world, you know, because my arms are not long enough to feel comfortable. I might have to start charging you for this, so how much are you going to pay me?" Hey, what can I say—she's her father's child, a true entrepreneur! I am sure that I also did mention that she is absolutely gorgeous didn't I? I'm just checking. Anyway, I call her Mommy's precious little angel or princess, depending on whether it's a regal day or she's simply resonating innocence regarding some false accusation or another from her brothers. It seems that princesses just can't get a break these days!

Special message to parents:

As I've looked at my journey thus far, I have pondered a few things. First I've thought about all of the thugs out there who were at one time babies, innocent with a clean slate, and I wonder what went wrong. I know that somebody loved them, and in most cases, it must have been parents, and then I wonder what critical difference reigned in their homes and I came up with this:

From the first time I looked at my older son, I realized that I had been charged with an immense responsibility and never since have I taken my task any less seriously. I took on a charge and an opportunity to form a life, personality, and character for a future citizen. That meant that everything that he did or said—and later the other two children—would be a strict representation of the adult he would become. If he was mean to another child, I never passed it off as him being just whatever age he was; if he was selfish, I never let it go, and if he complained about others not liking him, I never saw it as an opportunity to blame them. Likewise, if his teacher gave him a bad grade, we never sat down and justified it. I always made sure he knew that in life there would be people that liked you and people that didn't, but that as long as you were making the effort to be the best person you could be towards those people, then it was their problem and not yours.

My children have been taught that it is wrong to lie, anytime, anywhere, for any reason, because it only just catches up to you anyway and the last person that you want to lie to is yourself because it is plain ridiculous for you to try and fool the one person who essentially "knows you best". They were told in no uncertain terms that it is wrong to steal and that even if you get extra change from a teller's or cashier's mistake, that it in no way means that God is watching over you and has blessed you with extra. You see, however tempting, I just don't believe God works like that.

My children have been taught to share and to give and to allow everyone their opinions and right to their own decisions, even when they disagree with them. That doesn't mean that they have to be friends with everyone but they know that they can be friends with those who are different, so long as they know their own identities and are strong enough to ensure that they are the influence—and not the other way around.

If parents love their children, they should love them enough to teach them the rules and laws of the world and not justify their wrongdoings or condone their bad behavior. When a child says, "My teacher does not like me," instead of assuming that because the teacher is old or short or black or white or Spanish or Jamaican, that the accusation must therefore be true because never forget that our prejudices do, after all, often get in the way. Instead, we should ask our child, "*Why do you feel that way?*" And if they get in trouble, ask them what they might have done to cause it.

We should take action every day to ensure that our future, via our children, is secure. We want to give something to society that it did not give to me: productive, self-supporting citizens of whom we can all be proud. Maybe if we all band together we can launch a new societal wave where "positive contributors can emerge"! Maybe that will be the critical difference.

Stop dragging certain people home and passing them off on family:

Because I am in the presence of Angels, I have to be vigilante at all times to ensure that I try to save all damsels in distress or whatever the male equivalent for damsel would be; however it does not mean I should be dragging them home. Of this I must always know the difference!

You'll be familiar with this concept if you saw the beginning of the movie *Soul Food*, when Terry made the statement to Maxine at Byrd and Lem's wedding—right as Lem was out there dancing with his ex. That saying has never left me, and of course it came right after I had enough of the trifling, ridiculous antics of some man who I felt I just had to save from himself. Of course, I eventually found out that if he couldn't save himself then I sure wouldn't have a chance in you-know-where to do so.

I understand that last statement clearly, but of course because I am also a woman and a mother, bleeding hearts just always seem to be pouring onto/into my daily routes. And sure enough, the saving, nurturing, and protecting quality with which we seem to come equipped comes to the fore, and before we know it, we seem to have "taken them home and passed them off on family." I say this hypothetically too, because sometimes we might not have actually taken them home, but "home" as in around close friends or other family members still counts. On occasion, of course, I have seen such childish, pouting; nitpicking, kicking-and-screaming selfishness that it becomes obvious even to me that he cannot be permitted to actually meet my brood until I can see that he has changed his behavior. My point is that *he* actually has to be worthy; it's not the other way around, because my brood only deserves the best.

Things I've Learned:

As the years have passed, new things have continued to dawn on me; new worries replaced the old ones. There is an old saying that when kids are young they hang on to your apron strings but when they get older they hang on to your heart. This new place seems to be home for the rest of their lives. Sometimes I just long for the apron string days because things were so much "simpler" then, only I couldn't seem to see it at the time.

When my younger son was fifteen, he told me he couldn't have this particular girl as his girlfriend anymore. He had this earnest look on his face and I could see his distress but when I asked him why, I found out that he had in fact noticed that I wasn't too keen on her! Yet, I could have sworn that I had done the most stellar job of concealing my feelings, but you see, clearly our kids know us as well as we know them! He went on to explain that he could not be happy if his family disapproved of someone that he was with and he realized that I was not happy.

I learned that it isn't fair to burden my kids and that I have to let them love who they will and hope that the sense that I have been trying so hard to instill in them will be active through the whole process. I just need to stand by and be there if and when they need me. This was reinforced at his graduation from middle school, as I sat there watching him from the end of the table, sitting with his girl, her mom, and her family since she had graduated that same night too. That was the beginning of me seeing him grow away from me and that it was a normal thing no matter how hard it seemed at the time. I remember looking at my son from across the other end of the table and thinking how life just seems to fly by and change, and how we are supposed to keep up with everything (all while trying to hold back the tears of course). His dad having noticed just consoled me with the words "you know you'll always be his best girl right"? To this day, I hope this is true, but I also know it may be a bit unrealistic and I might have to compromise and share the "best girl" title one day. I guess all I can say is that I sure hope she is worthy.

At sixteen, my older son who often has these grand epiphanies, said to me, "Mom, you know you were right?" He reminded me that I had told his brother and he that one day their friends would think their sister was pretty and that hearing that would bother them. He said it had actually happened like that recently and that it had felt really weird. His brother chimed in that it was just a kid "about her age" so I should not panic, but they had already "dealt with it" by quarantining her off into another room any time another male was around. So, I've learned that our kids do actually realize when we are right and that although we don't think they are listening, they really are!

I remember when my daughter was about six, she used to ask me all the time, "Mommy, am I going to have boobies like you one day?" and I would tell her that yes, she would, but that they would be more beautiful than mine. She would respond, "I want them to be just like yours because yours are beautiful, Mommy." Then, a few years later when she was about nine, she looked at me when we were in the bathroom together and asked again, "Mommy, are my boobies going to look like that when I grow up?" but in a completely opposite tone and with a totally different expression on her face. I haughtily told her that they wouldn't unless she had three children and breastfed them for umpteen years, since feeding them naturally sacrificed a woman from ever looking like a normal human being again! I don't think she got the sarcasm or was left on any guilt trip, since the only thing I saw on her innocent face was simple relief!

So again, I've learned that there comes a time in every woman's life when our daughter will not think we are as beautiful as she did when she was small, because by now, she is the beautiful one—and both you and she know it. But I've also learned that even though I feel she no longer thinks I'm perfect, when she's around others she actually does, and she tells them so too. In short, I've learned that no matter how great or rotten I am, my kids love me desperately, so for their sake I should always be on my best behavior.

My kids tell me that I talk too loud and get upset too quick at them when I disagree about anything. I blame it on being a "McLaughlin" woman; we all get loud for no reason at all when we want to get our point across. My father's sisters are also really animated, so I also blame it on them. My kids don't buy it, of course, but what I've learned is that if I quiet down, they *will* talk and tell me what they are feeling.

I've learned that I should listen to my kids, because they actually do know me almost as well as I know them and they also know what they're talking about. And also like me, they have my best interest at heart.

I've learned that a family is a team and that you are only as good as the other members and your own ability to be a team player. Yes, I *am* the head of this team—but all members are equally important.

You know what I really learned though; I've learned that my kids are almost as smart as I am!

One set of footprints:

As I progressed on my journey, I came to understand that I have not been alone and I don't mean the family, friends, and support system. When I think of where I would be today had I really been alone, I often shudder. Sometimes, I look around to see if anyone is watching as I speed through life with its many responsibilities, as I plow down doors and bound into places unannounced and unapologetic. I walk alone in valleys, at times, on mountain tops at other times and I often feel the sweet brush of comfort. Comfort like a reassuring whisper that propels me along my way and guiding my steps. Whispering to me at all times to be patient with others and myself, to regroup and start over sometimes and to be cautious about my affairs bearing in mind always that I am somebody's mama and I should always act accordingly.

When I look at my achievements, I think about the fact that I am a simple girl, from a simple world, and I know that only by faith have I been able to come this far. In 1994, I left my husband, took my three little kids in tow, with only one year of college under my belt. I left marital "security" not knowing how I'd be able to manage to pay rent and survive for the next decade or so.

Today, I am educated and have my own home and a worthwhile profession that I am so proud to be a part of. I thank God that I still have my kids in tow; well they seem to tower over me now but they are still by my side and I am so proud of the people that they are becoming. I have great friends and a great life and although I have often wondered what could possess me to write a story about my life, I then think, like my daughter in her 11 year old wisdom once said; "I like my life, that's why."

Today, I am proud of the one set of footprints that have carried me all this way, free of charge, and I know I am not that light a load. I thank God for blessing me along my journey with my babies: DJ, Richie, and Caitlin. I count it all joy, and today I can smile and say that with God's help, I did it, I really did!

PART III

Changing the dream

Taking a dream by the hand is sometimes a necessary tool for actualization.

As I look back at my experiences, I see that there have been many doors that I have had to kick open, armed with a baby bag on one shoulder, a baby on each hip, and a stroller in front of me, charging past and through signs that say "No pets" and "No kids," and other doors that say "Sick days only count for you, not applicable if your kid is sick." I have had to fight so many of the stereotypes to which people subscribe when they see you carrying two kids and pushing a third; it seems that you just have to fight or you'll get lost in the shuffle.

I remember thinking how nice it would be to find someone to love me and take care of me and my kids. I remember wishing and praying every night that this would happen, only to wake up to see that it hadn't. I remember meeting men who told me, "If only it wasn't for your kids," that I finally understood that my dream was unlikely to materialize any time soon. But mostly, I remember waking up every day and getting on with the business of surviving and succeeding and taking care of those children who, by George, depended on it and never doubted whether I could do it or not.

I also remember waking up, not just to realize that another day had passed and I had done ok and I realized that I had done this on my own, well God and me anyway. Somewhere in the middle of hoping someone would come and rescue me, I had simply rescued myself. That old dream of a knight in shining armor had been shelved, and while I would look at it from time to time, I never even realized how much time had passed by. One day recently, I looked in the mirror and the face I saw staring back was no longer that of the little girl from way back then; I realized for the first time that the years had actually gone by.

Sometimes I seem jaded; sometimes men have been scared of me because I'm too forward or strong. Maybe I *am* a little scary: I know what I want and I won't settle for anything less than the best. I don't need someone to save me! Hey, I sure sound scary, but all I know is that if I had not been all of these things with my three little kids in tow, I can't imagine where I would be today, or where they would be, for that matter!

There was a time in my life when I would enter a room and feel like I was the same as any other young, single, woman there, but I also knew that as long as I didn't reveal that I had three kids, then I would be treated the same as they were by the men. I understood that once I spoke about them, the impact that the information made would visibly not be in my favor. Of course, by looking at me, no one would ever have guessed that I had even one child, so, looking back, in all fairness the shock was often justified. I actually appreciated men who were honest enough to tell me that they were not interested in having a ready-made family or were not ready for all that responsibility. It hands-down beat the ones who tried to fool me to get me into the sack or those who tried to mooch off me, or fix my life because I hadn't even heard it was broken.

For a time, it was like I had this secret that if revealed at an inopportune time could be disastrous; sometimes anticipation of the actual revelation would cause me distress; other times I could wield the information like a grenade. Those were the times that brought me resolve and strength, to the point that when I entered a room it would be with self-image so intact that no one present could any longer make me feel small. I had eventually arrived. I was somebody special, and as for those who didn't think I was spectacular, well, I had accepted that they had the problem anyway.

Nowadays, I enter a room not looking for anyone or anything; I just know I have the same rights as anyone else to be there. When my "secret is revealed" today, there can only be one valid response: reverence at what I have accomplished regarding my charge to rear three kids in this world. I get respect and a hush—maybe the latter exists only in my head—but it's there; a hush that simply whispers, "There is Somebody's Mama." My life means something to at least three people and that means everything to me.

Nowadays, a man can't even try to impress me, he can only just be himself, be kind, giving and loving and then just hope for the best, because I am so impressed with myself and what I have done with my life that he really has to have some story to really impress me anyway.

The dream of being saved by someone has been firmly shelved. It has not been looked at for a long time because the process of wanting and waiting to be saved turned into me saving myself. In fact, I think that now it is time to dust off that dream, frame it as a memento of the years, and sit it on my mantle, because no longer does it make me feel sad or bitter. Now I am happy for those days because they were the days when I was tested and discovered I could survive. They made me who I am today and I am really proud of that.

For all the other women on this "lone ranger" path, I simply wish for you the love and self-acceptance of yourself on your journey. I wish for you the understanding to recognize that you are not alone, just charged with the worthy task of shaping the future of tomorrow. I wish for you the conviction that you can do it without a man, but I also wish for you patience to wait for him to find you.

But most of all I wish for you forgiveness for your mistakes and the knowledge that you have to be kind to you and then the world will have to follow suit. And while on this quest, may you find the strength to believe in yourself and your ability to change your dreams.

Acknowledgments

To my children, David, Richard, and Caitlin Tyson, because you make me know how blessed I am each day that I live. You are my world and make everything worthwhile.

To my sister, Jamie: My sister, my daughter, my very best friend. Through the years you showed me what true love is and continue to teach me what it means to be a true friend and how to stay in someone's corner. You have walked this journey with me, defending me when you had to and running away demons, even good ones sometimes, and just knowing that I could do it all.

To my mom, Aida, who taught me how a mother should love her kids by showing me. You were my first example. You inspire me every day to get it right.

To my great-grandmother, Catherine Valree, for loving me so much, it never hurt!

To my sisters and brothers who make me know I am never alone.

To my brother, Ercely, for thinking I am the perfect woman; tell your friends! Then again—maybe not!

Thanks to my old friend Shana who told me that I should write a book and I did; hopefully you were right....eh heh!

To my friend, Anita, who thinks I am perfect and never lets me tell her differently....and then she wrote me!

To my friend, Lucille, for always laughing at my jokes, and for staying in my corner even though it can often mean trouble.

To Mernelyn, for being there through the hard times, for being my friend and true confidante, even when I know you wanted to get a life.

To Francis, for being such a wonderful friend, for believing in me and encouraging me to go forward with this book. My very first fan. ... Whoever would have known?

To Michelle for helping me make the first step towards seeing my words in print.

To Wosila for putting it together.

To Colin for helping me to find my flow and hopefully we can now call it a book!!

To Tommy for finding me amongst the chaos; however did that happen?

And to Des, for believing in this project, working for free, and being what I needed most, a bossy chick. ... Without you, where would I be today? How about lunch in S.A.....soon???

And Especially

To Dabo, for giving me three precious lives and for all that you did, the best way you knew how. My regrets are few and my sorrow is immeasurable!

About the Author

Courtesy of Rainbow Photo

Catherine is a qualified counselor in the human services field. She teaches and conducts self development workshops on her spare time.

She lives with her three children in the beautiful Cayman Islands and Miami Florida.

For more information on upcoming books or projects, check out her website at www.somebodysmama.com.

Printed in the United States
220626BV00002B/3/P